RESTORATION STORY

WHY JESUS MATTERS IN A BROKEN WORLD

Robert K. Cheong

New
Growth
Press

newgrowthpress.com

New Growth Press, Greensboro, NC 27401
newgrowthpress.com
Copyright © 2021 by Robert K. Cheong

Cover Design: Faceout Books, faceoutstudio.com
Interior Design and Typesetting: Gretchen Logterman

ISBN: 978-1-64507-165-5 (Print)
ISBN: 978-1-64507-166-2 (eBook)

Library of Congress Cataloging-in-Publication Data
Names: Cheong, Robert K., author.
Title: Restoration story : why Jesus matters in a broken world / Robert K. Cheong.
Description: Greensboro, NC : New Growth Press, [2021] | Includes bibliographical references and index. | Summary: "Some of us struggle to find meaning or identity, and all of us want to be loved. But God has a story too"-- Provided by publisher.
Identifiers: LCCN 2021022379 (print) | LCCN 2021022380 (ebook) | ISBN 9781645071655 (print) | ISBN 9781645071662 (ebook)
Subjects: LCSH: Regeneration (Theology) | Storytelling--Religious aspects--Christianity.
Classification: LCC BT790 .C44 2021 (print) | LCC BT790 (ebook) | DDC 234/.4--dc23
LC record available at https://lccn.loc.gov/2021022379
LC ebook record available at https://lccn.loc.gov/2021022380

Printed in the United States of America
28 27 26 25 24 23 22 21   1 2 3 4 5

"The best thing about *Restoration Story* is that it is both biblically faithful and gospel-centered. But that's not all that excites me; this book is field tested by men and women with a wide range of ages, ethnicities, and Christian experiences. Moreover, Dr. Cheong has created a reproducible model that doesn't require experts to lead. This work will help pastors and leaders disciple people to care for one another how Jesus and the apostles envisioned. I highly recommend you reading, learning, and reproducing what is taught in this book, as I've seen firsthand the profound impact that it has had on our church members."

Jamaal Williams, Lead Pastor, Sojourn Church Midtown; president, Harbor Network

"*Restoration Story* is a gospel feast and will prove to be a most helpful aid in discipling believers, equipping leaders, resourcing cohorts, and aiding counselors. Robert Cheong invites us to find our place in God's story as both characters and messengers— doing the heart work of spiritual formation. He understands the narrative nature of growth in Christ, taking us through the four-fold plotline of the Bible: Creation, Fall, Redemption, and Consummation. So well written and creatively illustrated, I will look forward to using this resource in my coaching ministry."

Scotty Smith, Pastor Emeritus, Christ Community Church, Franklin, TN; teacher-in-residence, West End Community Church, Nashville, TN

"Forged in the trenches of pastoral ministry and written from a deep belief in the power of Christ for personal transformation, *Restoration Story* is a fresh resource for pastors and ministry leaders to use in their local churches as they work with men and women desiring to see God, his Word, and his people transform their lives. I've seen the fruit of this firsthand as a pastor at Sojourn Midtown and throughout our network of churches."

Dave Owens, Executive Director, Harbor Network

"I have always been sharpened from co-laboring with Robert and find his teaching to be clear and deeply rooted in an abiding love of God, his Word, and the people of God found in the church everywhere. As one who works with the church on a global level, I have seen that Robert's insights, being from the Word, transcend cultural boundaries and are accessible and revolutionary to people everywhere. I heartily recommend Robert's book as an invaluable resource for anyone desiring to lead communities of faith into greater love of the Savior."

Paul Athanasius, Cross-cultural worker and trainer

"As a Christian and a pastor, I've been so encouraged by how many people have benefited from Robert's work. Personally, it has blessed me as I have learned what it means to be cared for by God and his church. As a pastor, it has transformed the way I preach to my church and how I engage in personal counseling. The beauty of it all is that I see people truly experiencing God."

Moe Hafeez, Family Pastor, Cornerstone Church, Atlanta, GA

"As a writer, I know firsthand how God has used the process of storytelling to challenge, heal, and cultivate my relationship with him. But for some shortsighted reason, I never thought how significant it might be for others. With *Restoration Story*, pastor Robert Cheong taps the power of storytelling for discipleship, inviting participants to find their personal stories in God's larger one. So pick up this book and discover a good, gracious Author, who's writing the story of his people even now."

Hannah Anderson, Author of *Humble Roots: How Humility Grounds and Nourishes Your Soul*

CONTENTS

INTRODUCTION

NO MATTER how many acquaintances we have, few relationships go really deep. People may know what we do for a living, how we tend to dress, what we like to eat, and maybe even where we just went on vacation—but that's all they know.

When it comes to being known, we feel a strange mix of need and fear. We may resist sharing with others what is going on in our hearts and lives, but we still long to be known. Often, we pull away from others because we feel like we're not like them; we isolate ourselves when others hurt us. Nevertheless, we still want to belong to a community. Even though we barely have enough time or energy to simply pay bills, eat and sleep, and engage at some level with friends and family, we still want a larger purpose in life.

Where do we go to find out who we really are? Where do we find satisfaction for our deepest longings?

You Aren't Alone: We All Have A Story

When you're struggling with self-doubt and loneliness, lacking direction and purpose, you may believe everyone

1

else is doing better than you. You might think you're the only one who is struggling. Even if you are aware of others battling through life in similar ways, it doesn't make your life any easier. The fact that others are dealing with similar issues doesn't relieve the weight of your weariness or mend the brokenness in your soul. In fact, being aware of others who are in the same boat as you can leave you feeling hopeless.

But the truth that our struggles are common does matter. When you understand that other people face difficulties like yours—when you grasp the reality that you are not alone—you should feel some relief. Knowing that others experience life in comparable ways can help you believe you are not alone. Such knowledge counters the lies you may believe in your fears and despair—the lies that have convinced you that there is something wrong with you or that you are different from other people.

Your Story Matters

Often, we don't stop to consider life beyond our daily routines, challenges, joys, disappointments, and longings.

Some may view life as an ever-unfolding series of unavoidable situations, feeling subject to fate and whatever the universe has in store. These people picture themselves caught in a river current that dictates where they go and how they live.

Others see themselves as the author of their story. They approach life like a mountain to be scaled, where they plan every move, preparing for the worst and hoping for the best. These people know they can't make the hike alone, so they surround themselves with trusted friends.

Everyone sees and approaches life somewhere along the spectrum between the river and the mountain.

As you face your own struggles, you can look for answers in your story, or you can seek direction apart from your story. Regardless, your story matters to God. He wants you to find answers, direction, and hope as you look at two very special, interconnected stories—your own story and God's story.

Your Story and God's Story

Whether you realize it or not, your story is lived out within God's bigger story. God knows every detail of your story. He knew every aspect of your life before you were born (Psalm 139:16). And he wants you to know him more fully through your story—not despite it.

God is the divine author of your story, but this doesn't mean that you have no choices. Instead, God creatively involves himself with your life, shaping it along the way.

But God's story is not only true beyond our imagination, it is different from all other stories. It is a story not only to be *told*, but a story to be *lived*. It doesn't just entertain us for a minute—it shapes how we live, how we love, and reveals to us God's plan for us. God's story reveals the most intimate relationship that we can ever know. Through our union with Christ, we can experience a perfect love that satisfies the deepest longings of our soul. It's only through knowing God and his story that our distorted understandings of love and relationships can be untangled. God invites us to abide in Christ through the school of life, as we journey through the dark valleys, the mountaintop experiences, and everything in between.

The Bible reveals a tapestry of real stories woven together to showcase the beautiful and redeeming narrative of God's story. God uses these stories to show us how he works through the details of our lives today. Through our own stories, he wants us to grasp the intangible realities of his comforting presence, the sustaining peace of his faithful promises, and the safety of his incomparable power. As we experience God in these ways, the life-giving dimensions of his love will compel us to no longer live for ourselves but to live for him.

What Journey Is God Inviting You to Take?

Understanding your story matters. God is not inviting you to endless introspection, to reexperience your past, or to relive your pain. Instead, God wants you to know and experience his nearness and goodness in the seemingly insignificant parts of your story. He wants to show you his tenderness and power in the significant moments of your story. God delights in restoring broken souls. He does this in his own time and ways as people live more and more from the reference point of his story. God wants you to understand the gospel story as a restoration story, where he restores your soul, your relationships, and ultimately, your God-given humanity.

His Story Informs and Transforms

God's story from Genesis to Revelation serves as a never-changing framework that will help you navigate life's storms. When it feels like you're drowning, God guides you through the chaos. When you find it easy to drift, he sets you upon his intended course. God's story not only captures the reality of life in this fallen world but, more importantly, reveals his reality and his heart for his people.

We can interpret reality based on our experiences and situation, but God invites us instead to live our story based on his. The goal of this book is to help you see how your story is embedded in God's story of restoration. God knows every twist and turn of your story, and he desires that you come to know him more intimately and experience his love more deeply as you live with him in his story. God wants to lift your eyes to him and his story as you follow Christ by faith and obedience. When we live out of God's story, he transforms how we love him and others.

As we journey through the stories of four individuals, you'll see how God's story reframes how they see their realities. As they learn to abide in the love of Christ, you'll see how he restores their souls, freeing them to love God and others in ways that reflect Christ. You'll also see how God redeems their stories despite unexpected twists and turns. Their stories will help you to apply God's story directly to your own and help you love and live differently.

God's Invitations

At the end of each chapter is a prompt to respond to God's invitation to draw near to him by reflecting on an assigned Bible passage. Spending time with God and reflecting on your story in light of God's story is an essential part of each chapter. This time of abiding in Christ will allow you to find rest for your soul and also learn to trust and obey him. Though these activities will take time and thought, participating in them will help you get the most out of this book and apply the concepts in each chapter to transform the way you view your reality.

As you read this book, I pray you'll begin to see how abiding in Christ enables you to know and experience God's love and how this intimate relationship serves as God's primary means of restoring your broken and weary soul. I pray that you'll experience firsthand why you need to draw near to God, not only during your time of need but as a way of life. My prayer is that you will grow more confident in Jesus Christ and that your joy in him would grow more and more full. God doesn't answer every question on this side of heaven, but instead, he gives you himself. Will you join him on this journey?

CHAPTER 1
REFRAMING OUR REALITY THROUGH THE LENS OF THE FALL

STEVE AND Emma bumped into each other in a crowded store. A quick apology led to a lingering look, which led to a long, enjoyable conversation over coffee. Through their daily phone calls and time spent together almost every weekend, they shared things about themselves that they rarely shared with others. Their relationship deepened over the next year, and they found themselves dreaming about a life together.

One day, Steve and Emma strolled through a park where they'd spent countless hours reading and relaxing together under their favorite tree. Just as he had rehearsed a hundred times in his mind, Steve stopped, got down on one knee, and said, "Emma, you are the love of my life. In the last year, you've taught me how to slow down and enjoy life. I've never laughed so much or felt so deeply loved. I can't imagine life without you. Will you marry me?" Emma squealed and jumped up and down as she shouted, "YES!"

Before long, the wedding was over and the newlyweds learned they both brought different expectations and relational baggage into their marriage. Their individual family upbringing and past experiences had combined to shape what each thought marriage would be like. Yet even though they argued like other couples, they seemed to be able to work through the issues one at a time, and this brought them closer.

The most painful challenge Steve and Emma faced during their first six years of marriage was infertility. In every other area of their marriage, they were growing, but in this one aspect they seemed to be sinking deeper into hopelessness. This wasn't what they had hoped for; this isn't how they saw their story going. Then, one bone-chilling winter evening, Steve arrived home from work, hung up his coat and scarf, and walked into their living room where Emma fell into his arms. With tears running down her cheeks, she whispered, "I feel like such a failure. We've tried for years and I still can't get pregnant."

Confronted with Emma's pain, Steve was speechless. He had no idea how to respond. They embraced and cried together.

Life and Relationships Are Hard

Fears and disappointments make life hard. In spite of our different circumstances, many of us struggle in similar ways. We want to be known, to belong, and to have purpose and identity, but our thoughts, emotions, and desires can serve as our frame of reference. When we are disappointed, those thoughts and emotions cause us to doubt our purpose and identity.

So we can turn to other people to affirm that identity. Whether we're outwardly boastful or inwardly insecure, we seem wired to look to others to give us what we think we need based on how we feel. We use others to advance our careers, manipulate others to win their affections, offer "love" as a ploy to be accepted and to be loved in return, or pull back from others for fear of being found out or being hurt again. When we relate to others, it is for the primary reason of self-interest or self-protection. But we will disappoint ourselves and others every time.

It's no wonder that relationships are hard. Almost everyone has experienced frustration and hurt in their relationships. We have been mistreated or unloved, ignored or neglected, lied to or wrongly accused, betrayed and belittled. When we experience these things again and again, we wonder, *Is it me?* or *Did I do something to deserve this treatment?*

Some of us have been abused or have witnessed unimaginable evil. Such experiences can leave a person traumatized, filled with fear and anxiety, and easily triggered by whatever may cause a flashback to these horrific encounters. For these reasons, life and relationships are not only hard, but they can be terrifying.

We need to be aware of the reality of evil in the world. But we also need to understand such realities within a larger story, a story filled with hope.

Our Realities Can Overshadow God's Bigger Reality

We often struggle with fixating on the most pressing, persistent, or painful realities. As a result, we can forget that there is more going on in life. You have an urgent deadline, so you spend all your waking hours evaluating the details, considering the different scenarios, preparing a proposal, and getting ready for the presentation. Or you may live in persistent pain. Some days, it's all you can do to get out of bed and get dressed. You can spend countless hours researching new treatments and listening to podcasts from those who claim to have alleviated the pain altogether. Or perhaps your mother's death has left you devastated. Your heart throbs with grief, and you find yourself sitting in regret, wishing you had spent more time with her, or, as you remember your last conversation, you wish you had said things differently.

It's good and right to have a full experience of what is going on in life, but these in-your-face realities can dominate our hearts and minds. They give us tunnel vision, where we cannot see anything else. It doesn't take long for us to forget about our families amid deadlines. It doesn't take long for chronic pain to define our lives. It doesn't take long for grief and regret to consume and drown us in despair. So how are we supposed to live in this fallen, broken world?

We need to understand there is more to our story than the most pressing and tangible realities.

On the one hand, this is something that comes naturally to us. As normal human beings, we instinctively seek to find meaning and purpose in life beyond our circumstances and relationships. But the problem comes when we seek that meaning in the wrong places. Even when people can see the forest in the midst of the trees, they miss recognizing that it is a forest in God's world.

In 2 Corinthians 4:4, God reminds us, "The god of this age has blinded the minds of unbelievers, so that they cannot see the light of the gospel that displays the glory of Christ." Addressing our human blindness is essential. Seeing our realities within God's bigger story makes a difference. The rest of this book examines how God's story impacts the way we live and love, but for now we will focus on how God's story helps us reframe our struggles within this fallen world.

We Experience Life Uniquely

During his forty-five-minute commute home on the train, Mark keeps to himself. The people around him are engrossed in books or phone conversations, working on their laptops, or relaxing with the music from their headphones drowning out the noise of the world. Mark takes the same route each day. He sits in the same seat, surrounded by mostly the same people. But he doesn't know anything about them, and no one knows what makes him unique either. No one else shares his exact DNA; no one else has his fingerprints; and no one else has the same biometric facial features.

Even beyond these differing physiological markers, each person encounters life in unique ways. People are distinct in the ways they perceive, interpret, and respond to various life experiences. When you're comforting a friend grieving the death of her father, it might not be helpful to say, "I know exactly how you feel, since I lost my father years ago." You do share a common experience, the death of a parent, but you don't necessarily know your friend's relationship with her dad. You don't know how her dad expressed, or didn't express, his love to her. She could be experiencing deep anger and sadness over a father whom she could never please. Or her father may have been an alcoholic who was belligerent towards everyone in the house when he was drunk. Or maybe her story with her father was good, while yours is different— your father was never around, and even when he was, you could always find him in the recliner watching sports on TV and clueless about what you were going through in life. So, in his death, you grieved, but not in the same way you would have if he had been more loving through his words and actions, and not in the same way your friend may be grieving.

As the cliché implies, no one can truly walk in your shoes. Your life can't be lived by anyone else, since you alone have experienced it. Only you can live and relive the glorious and the painful parts of your story.

Yet What We Experience Is Similar

Despite our unique physiological traits and personal experiences, we do share some similar realities with the other seven billion people who live in the world.

Nikki shares physiological and anatomical commonalities with other women in the world. Growing up in the United Kingdom, she shared the same school systems, a love for fish and chips, and some of the same seaside holiday destinations with her family and friends. Nikki has also discovered that many of her friends, whether Brits or Americans, enjoy hanging out at pubs or bars to relax and have a good time. She's noticed that regardless of what country she is in, she will see people glued to their phones, scrolling through their social media feeds. She has also realized that people are people regardless of where they live; and they share the same anxieties about dating, careers, and navigating life's uncertainties.

We are unique, yet we share common traits and experiences, regardless of who we are and where we live. This reality points to something that King Solomon wrote some three thousand years ago: "There is nothing new under the sun" (Ecclesiastes 1:9b).

Do you agree with Solomon when you consider things like the technological advances of the internet, cell phones, planes, self-driving cars, and artificial intelligence? What about the cutting-edge medical research that has pushed back the borders of various diseases? These seem like radically new things—but aspects of life such as birth, work, marriage, and death, never change; and humanity's fundamental struggles remain the same.[1] The apostle Paul wrote, "No temptation has overtaken you except what is common to mankind" (1 Corinthians 10:13).

The good news is that Jesus Christ has been, and always will be, the ultimate source of hope and relief for the repeated problems of humankind throughout generations. Everything else will come and go, rise and fall, but God remains the same in the past, present, and future, even into eternity.

If it is true that there is nothing new under the sun, then we can reframe how we see and understand our struggles. They aren't something new. But why are these struggles so common? God's story shows us the answer.

Common Struggles Emerge from the Fall

God's story reveals the gospel of Jesus Christ through four major movements—*creation, fall, redemption,* and *consummation*—each of which will be unpacked in subsequent chapters. God's story serves as an invaluable framework to help us understand the world, ourselves, and God. This story is revealed in Scripture.

The Bible tells us that God didn't create us to struggle with life, but to live in peace with him. God didn't create us to be driven by our work, but by his love. God didn't create us to experience loneliness and to live without a sense of purpose, but to live for him. God didn't create us to experience the pain and sorrow of infertility but to be fruitful and multiply.

So, if God didn't create us for such struggles, why do we struggle in these and so many other ways?

The Bible tells us that God's perfect creation was distorted and disordered when the first man and woman sinned against God. Humanity's sin and rebellion against its Creator unleashed the never-ending destruction of evil upon God's good world. Disasters like earthquakes kill thousands in crumbling buildings, and tsunamis drown countless others, plunging families and friends into deep despair and anguish over the loss of life and property.

Evil also disorders our souls and our relationships in a particular way through common struggles. We see these common struggles rooted in the story of the fall when the first man and woman, Adam and Eve, disobeyed God.

In Genesis 3, the devil, disguised as a serpent, tempted our first parents through *fantasy*, enticing them to envision a life where they did not have to trust or obey God or his Word. He also planted the idea that by eating the fruit, they could be like God. Fantasy means refusing to accept or address your actual situation, instead seeking a different reality that offers an imagined escape or hope. Adam and Eve were deceived into believing the serpent's lies, and they trusted in their own understanding rather than the wisdom of God.

As soon as their desire to please themselves overpowered their desire to please God, they bit the forbidden fruit and experienced *guilt* before a holy God. Guilt is pain that comes from something you've done wrong. Our first parents knew they had done evil in God's eyes.

Before their disobedience, Adam and Eve were naked and not ashamed; but in their sin, they were filled with *shame* in God's presence and tried to cover their nakedness with fig leaves. Shame is pain that comes from who you are or who you think you are. The man and woman sensed they were different from how God created them to be.

As soon as they heard God approaching in the garden, Adam and Eve hid; they were afraid because of their nakedness. Their *fear* caused them to hide from God rather than draw near to him. Fear is an anxious anticipation of something perceived to be threatening or dangerous. Adam and Eve saw God as a threat rather than as a refuge.

When God asked the man what had happened, the man responded with bitterness and blame: "'The woman *you* put here with me—*she* gave me some fruit from the tree, and I ate it'" (Genesis 3:12, emphasis mine). You might say his response reflected *anger* against God and the woman. Anger is a strong feeling of displeasure or hostility in response to someone or something that opposes what you value.[2] Adam saw God and the woman standing in the way of what he valued, and he responded accordingly.

The last common struggle is *sorrow,* which is a deep sadness or despair, usually resulting from loss. The man and woman experienced sadness when they lost their right relationship with God in their sin. They also experienced despair when God declared his punishment to each of them. But the ultimate sorrow they experienced was when God banished them from his presence and placed cherubim with a flashing sword to keep them from reentering the garden to reach the tree of life.

Every person in this world struggles in these and other ways for one significant reason: *We were not created to know and experience evil.* How do we know this? Because the one thing that God prohibited the first man and woman from doing was eating from the tree of the knowledge of good and evil. Ever since their personal disobedience exploded into a global pandemic of sin, evil has overwhelmed and overpowered us in every aspect of life. This includes both our body and souls.

Common Struggles Are a Response to Evil

Common struggles—fantasy, guilt, shame, fear, anger, sorrow, etc.—should not be understood as our core sins. God created us with the ability to dream and imagine possibilities beyond our current realities. But those dreams can be twisted when we struggle with false guilt for thinking we should have or could have done something differently. We can experience shame not from our own sin, but from how others treat us, like Jesus when he was shamed on the cross. God not only created us to fear him but also to be alert and avoid danger. Jesus experienced righteous anger, and so can we, even though, for us, such anger can quickly morph into sinful anger. It's natural to experience sorrow over loss, so much so that Jesus was called a "man of sorrows" (Isaiah 53:3 ESV).

Common struggles are my way of describing how we respond to the evil in and around us that has resulted from the fall. Such struggles can be both passive and active; the responses flow from our thoughts, emotions, and desires as we relate to the people and circumstances around us. These common struggles are not sinful, but they become sinful when they drive us more than faith, and when they keep us from loving God and others. Our common struggles become sinful when they overshadow God and compel us to live in ways contrary to how God created us to live.

Common Struggles Coexist

Nikki finds herself *fantasizing* about becoming a partner in her growing marketing firm. She has sacrificed her personal life in an attempt to gain an edge over her peers. Whenever Nikki is between projects, she will take time off to catch her breath and rest her worn-out body and mind. However, in these slow times she is often plagued by *guilt* for not traveling to see her mom, whom she hasn't seen in three years. When she sits in silence at home, Nikki struggles with a sense of inadequacy, or *shame*, as she compares herself with those around her. She can be overcome by *fear* and *anxiety*, believing she is all alone. This constellation of struggles often drags her into a deep, lingering *sorrow*.

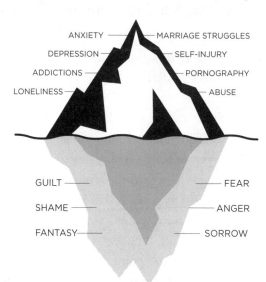

Mark seeks to counter his loneliness by escaping into *fantasy* through video games. He has bragging rights with his teammates around the world—some of whom admit they spend hours playing to avoid the sad and hard realities of life. Mark finds some comfort in knowing that he is not the only one who struggles with loneliness and purpose in life. Still, such knowledge doesn't ease the *sorrow* and *shame* that comes with those struggles.

It's important to know that common struggles coexist. We can think about them like primary colors that mix together to make all the different colors. Each of these common struggles can combine with others to create distinct difficulties in your life. As these struggles combine, they can create surges of pain and confusion that toss us back and forth, pushing us underwater like the ocean waves.

Common Struggles Lead to Relational Struggles

Because God created us for relationships, everything that impacts us also impacts how we relate to others. Emma's *shame* and her insatiable desire to be a mother has made her quieter around her coworkers, especially when they talk about their children. She finds it hard to rejoice when friends share they are pregnant. Emma finds herself dwelling more on the *sorrow* of her infertility than on the exciting news of life. She can even judge those around her as she tries to justify that she is just as good as those who have babies. Her close friends, who have grieved with her, have shared with her that they feel like they are walking on eggshells when they're with her, to the point where they hesitate to talk about their children. Emma's friendships have suffered.

Steve and Emma's struggle with infertility has put a strain on their marriage as well. Sexual intimacy feels more like an obligation than a pleasure. Steve struggles to know how he can help Emma. Month after month, pregnancy tests are negative, and she is *sorrowful* and depressed for days afterwards. Steve and Emma often find themselves impatient, *angry,* and harsh with one another when they try to have meaningful conversations. Steve is exhausted. Emma is not the woman he married. He finds himself *fantasizing* about a coworker who makes him laugh. At least he can talk about anything with her.

Our common struggles not only make our individual lives difficult, but they also make relationships complicated. With Emma and Steve, we see how these struggles are straining their relationship. We also see how the struggles have affected their relationship with God and given birth to sin. The sorrow and fantasy that Emma and Steve are engaging in are causing them to withdraw from God.

Reframing Our Struggles

It is helpful to reframe our struggles in light of the fall. If we are convinced that our common and relational struggles are the result of the fall, then we can have hope.

Why? First, the fall is not the end of God's story. Second, since our story is part of God's story, our struggles can be explained as being the result of evil defiling and distorting everything God made for good. Third, if our struggles can be reframed within the fall, then Christ's life, death, and resurrection are relevant to our struggles. We will see later how Christ came not only to reconcile us to God, but also to restore our souls damaged by evil. If we don't see our struggles in light of God's story, we can be confused about their cause, and discouraged from thinking that God can even help.

In the next chapter, we will look at why we need to work through our stories. We will see that a practical way of engaging in spiritual warfare is understanding how the various events and experiences in our lives have shaped how we see our lives. And we'll discover that such understanding comes primarily from the intentional work of discipleship.

God's Invitation

Spend some time in God's Word. Open your heart to God about your own experience with listening to and obeying his Word.

Read Genesis 3 and reflect on how you can see yourself through the thoughts, emotions, desires, and actions of the first man and woman. Can you relate to the common struggles they faced? Where do you see God's mercy and grace amid the first man and woman's sin against him?

CHAPTER 2
FACING YOUR REALITY THROUGH YOUR STORY

HAVE YOU ever been to the beach and enjoyed relaxing in the water on a foam board or inflatable float? You can spend countless hours floating, listening to the sound of the surf, rocking with the waves' rhythmic motions, and feeling the heat of the sun while the cool water laps on your arms and legs. But after some time of resting your eyes, you look up and suddenly realize that you have drifted far from where you started. You quickly scan the beach for your family, frantically looking for familiar faces and belongings.

Similarly, we can be swept along by the currents of life. It's not often that we slow down enough to reflect. We might evaluate our lives at a funeral or after a frightening experience that caused our life to "flash before our eyes." But, like our tendency to drift while resting on a float, more often we sadly look up and ask, "How did I get here?"

How Well Do You Know Your Story?

Your story is simply the events and experiences of your life that shape and inform how you know and interpret your circumstances and relationships. Said more concisely, your story captures the events and experiences that form who you are and how you live.

Though you've lived the moments of your life first-hand, you can experience them without knowing your story. There are several ways this can happen.

You can live *distracted*, preoccupied with the present demands of work and family while being swept up in hours of entertainment and recreation, food, and drink.

You can *live in the future*, continually rewriting the next chapter of your story to compensate for the pain and disappointment of the last. You convince yourself things will get better when this or that happens. You place your hope in changing circumstances.

You can *deny* parts of your story, trying to forget the chaos, loss, regret, rejection, or even the abuse that makes you feel unloved and unlovable. You may even suppress such realities because the shame or disappointment is too painful.

You can be *consumed* by your story, unable to move forward because the past seems so overwhelming. You see yourself mainly through the lens of your deep suffering or dark sin. Or, you may overidentify with the "good ole days," wanting to recreate or preserve them.

Getting Lost in Your Story

Nikki has lived consumed by her story. Her parents divorced when she was five years old. She always thought her parents loved each other until one day her mother sat her down and explained that she and her dad would be living in different apartments. Her mom reassured her that they still both loved her, and Nikki would get to see them both as if nothing had changed. However, working two jobs, her mom was busy and things between them did change—a distance opened up. Nikki's most vivid memory of growing up was being shuttled between her parents' places. She would often lose clothing, toys, or school assignments with all the back and forth. When her mom started dating, their relationship became even more strained.

Nikki remembers always feeling bitter towards her parents for having failed her. She felt abandoned by them and has struggled with trusting anyone after the divorce. Her story is full of guilt and sorrow. She wonders whether her parents would have stayed married if she would have been a better child. Because of the hardships and heartache she experienced during those years, Nikki vowed that she would never get a divorce. Living in the shadows of her parents' divorce has overwhelmed her life and affected how she views others, making it difficult for her to move forward and see her story clearly.

Why Do We Need to Know Our Story?

There are a couple of ditches that you can fall into if you don't work through your story. One is being endlessly preoccupied with trying to figure out *who you are* and *why you do what you do*. If you're trying to find those answers only within your own story, you will go around and around, like a dog chasing its tail.

On the other hand, if you try to avoid working through your story, unresolved issues can stunt your growth and squeeze out your joy. Like Nikki, you may get stuck in patterns of fear and distrust, or your life may be hijacked by reckless abandon as you try to escape the questions and confusion that swarm in your soul. As you consider the possibility of working through your story, you might ask, "How will this benefit me?" or "Will this be worth my time and discomfort?" These are valid questions.

We must acknowledge that working through our story can be painful. The obvious reason is that we may have to face the painful realities of our past. We can be reminded of embarrassing or regrettable things we have done. We can also grieve the loss of those we loved, or dreams that will never be.

But we need to work through our story because evil seeks to undermine God's purposes and plans. Leaving our stories untouched gives Satan ample ammo. The Enemy leverages the evil that we were never meant to experience in three main ways in our lives:

- *Evil can distort our vision.* Our story shapes how we see and understand our lives and relationships. As a result, our story can warp how we live and how we love both God and others.

- *Evil damages our souls.* The evil we experience—whether from ourselves, others, or the world around us—leaves us broken. We struggle with shame, guilt, fear, anger, and sorrow. In response, we may fantasize about or hope in things we believe will change how we think and feel about ourselves, ease the pain, or change our circumstances.

- *Evil can define our story.* As a result of our difficulty and hurtful life experiences and relationships, we can grow weary, merely trying to survive. We may respond to repeated disappointments by becoming cynical. We can even reach a point where we believe that life is not worth living or we will never know love.

Every encounter with evil brings disorder to our heart, soul, and mind. If we're to be "wise as serpents and innocent as doves" (Matthew 10:16 ESV), we must understand that this is part of an invisible but ever-present and all-too-real spiritual battle. To keep the enemy from outwitting us (2 Corinthians 2:11) and gaining a foothold (Ephesians 4:27), we must engage God in prayer as we work through our story. Whether you realize it or not, working through key moments and seasons of your life with an awareness of God's presence is a practical and personal way of engaging in spiritual warfare.

Understanding your story is not the goal. *But working through relevant parts of your story is the means of knowing and experiencing God more intimately through his story.*

God is not inviting you to face your story alone. Instead, God invites you to face parts of your story as you face him.

God also is not calling you to address everything in your past. In his own time, he will reveal those experiences that he wants to redeem. God has the power to restore the brokenness in your soul and empower you to experience the fullness of his love.

Why Do We Need to Look at God's Story?

God's story reminds us that we live in God's world, where Jesus rules and reigns. God's story informs and forms who we are and shows us how we are to live and love. God's story also counteracts the impact of evil in our hearts and lives.

God's story *reframes* how we see and understand life and relationships distorted by evil. He does this through his Word, so we begin to see life with his eyes and understand it with his heart.

God's story *restores* the soul that has been damaged by evil. As we abide in Christ, we come to know and experience his love, joy, peace, strength, and mercy. Beauty rises from the ashes. Life infuses our withered soul; mourning turns to joy; and his love resuscitates our soul. God frees us to love him with our entire being and to love others so they may taste and see that the Lord is good. God created our souls to respond to love with love.

God's story *redeems* stories that have been defined by evil. He shows us how he takes the events and experiences meant for evil and uses them for good. He uses the evil done to us to draw us near so that we can know and experience his love more deeply and personally. He uses the evil we have done to humble us and to show us our tendency to trust in our own understanding and push away the very life and love for which we were created. God's love shapes how we live and who we live for. As God's love compels us to live with him and for him, our story will be redeemed as it aligns with his story.

Joseph's Story

By examining the story of Joseph in Genesis, we see how looking at God's story can transform an individual's story.

Betrayed, Exiled, Enslaved, Accused, Imprisoned, and Forgotten

Joseph was the eleventh of Jacob's twelve sons. The drama starts when Jacob's preferential treatment of Joseph stirs

up envy in his older brothers (Genesis 37:3). Adding fuel
to their envy, Joseph recounts dreams that show he will
one day rule over his brothers and that they will bow down
before him. In their anger and jealousy, the brothers devise
a scheme to get rid of Joseph. They gang up on him, throw
him into a well, and then sell him to traveling merchants.
The brothers take Joseph's robe, dip it goat's blood, and
tell Jacob that a ferocious animal has devoured his favorite
son. Meanwhile, the traveling merchants sell Joseph to a
rich Egyptian named Potiphar, who is captain of Pharaoh's
guard.

In spite of his father's favoritism, Joseph's pride, and all
his brothers do to harm him in response, God is with Joseph so that he prospers in Potiphar's house (Genesis 39:2).
Potiphar puts Joseph in charge of everything he owns. But
even there, Joseph isn't free from evil. Potiphar's wife attempts to seduce Joseph twice. Both times he refuses because of his faithfulness to Potiphar and to God. Spurned,
Potiphar's wife accuses Joseph of trying to rape her. As a
result, Joseph is thrown into prison.

And yet, in the midst of Joseph's suffering, God shows
him "kindness" and grants him "favor in the eyes of the
prison warden" (Genesis 39:21). In prison, Joseph meets
Pharaoh's cupbearer and chief baker, both of whom had
been imprisoned for offending their master. Joseph inter-
prets their strange dreams, and predicts their fates. The
baker is punished for his crimes, but the cupbearer is set
free. Joseph asks the cupbearer to remember him and to
tell Pharaoh about his innocence so that he can be released
from prison. But in spite of his kindness to the cupbearer,

Joseph once again encounters evil. As soon as the cupbearer is released, he forgets all about Joseph.

Two years pass and Pharaoh has a dream that no one can interpret. At that moment the cupbearer finally remembers Joseph. He tells Pharaoh how Joseph had correctly interpreted his dream. So, Pharaoh calls for Joseph who tells him what his dream means, saying, "God has revealed . . . what he is about to do" (Genesis 41:25). Joseph says that God would bring seven years of abundance followed by seven years of famine. Seeing his discernment and wisdom, Pharaoh then places Joseph in charge of his palace and his people. Joseph stores up huge quantities of grain for Egypt during the seven years of abundance. During this time, he marries and has two sons. He names his first son Manasseh, because "God has made me forget all my trouble and all my father's household." He names the second, Ephraim because "God has made me fruitful in the land of my suffering" (Genesis 41:51–52).

Joseph's Response to the Evil He Has Endured

When the seven years of famine hit, Joseph begins to sell the stored grain. People from all over the world come to Egypt to buy it. When Jacob's family runs out of food, he sends ten of his sons to buy grain in Egypt. During a second trip for food, Joseph reveals his identity to his brothers and asks them to tell his father that he was alive. Then he invites his entire family to come and live in Egypt.

Jacob's family lives there for seventeen years before his death (Genesis 46–49). But when Jacob dies, Joseph's brothers fear for their lives. They worry that Joseph—now powerful and without his old father to restrain him—will take his revenge on them for how they'd treated him so many years ago. But Joseph surprises his brothers by telling them not to be afraid. Continuing, he says, "As for you, you meant evil against me, but God meant it for good, to bring it about that many people should be kept alive, as they are today" (Genesis 50:20 ESV).

The story of Joseph concludes with a scene in which several generations of children and grandchildren gather around Joseph's deathbed. In his last recorded words at 110 years old, Joseph says with confidence, "I am about to die. But God will surely come to your aid and take you up out of this land to the land he promised on oath to Abraham, Isaac and Jacob" (Genesis 50:24).

Joseph has been able to live with confidence in God, despite having been betrayed, exiled, enslaved, wrongly accused, and imprisoned. He knows God has always been with him. He testifies to God's faithfulness throughout his life.

If Joseph had focused on *his* story of injustice, oppression, and suffering, he would have remained a victim, and his relationship with God would have suffered. But by keeping his eyes on God and his faith in him, Joseph experiences the Lord's kindness and favor. He sees God's bigger story. God not only reframes how Joseph sees and experiences life but also restores the brokenness in his soul—God redeems Joseph's story.

God was glorified through the fruitfulness of Joseph's life. And Joseph's account is only one of countless stories of real people like you and me who transcended the darkness of their narratives through trusting and following God.

The 50:20 Principle

Steve and Emma spent countless hours hanging out in coffee shops and diners during their year of dating. They talked about every topic that came to mind as they sipped coffee and enjoyed their favorite meals. It was common for them to get lost in their conversations—to the point that restaurant staff would sometimes ask them to leave to make room for other customers. When this happened, they simply continued the conversation on their walk home. On their dates, Steve and Emma talked a lot about their family experiences growing up.

Steve grew up in a single-parent home. His mother worked hard at everything she did. She was a foreman at a local manufacturing company, and she oversaw a crew of twenty women and men on the second shift. His mom would awaken Steve every morning with a kiss on the forehead as she playfully pulled the covers off him. By the time he dragged himself out of bed, dressed, and combed his hair, she would have a hot breakfast with a big glass of juice waiting for him. His mom was gone when Steve got home from school and he was asleep by the time she got home from work, so they enjoyed their time together each morning, sharing highlights from the day before. They cracked jokes and would even cry together as she would take the time to listen and ask him questions about whatever challenges he faced.

After hearing about the great relationship Steve had with his mom, Emma shared that her family rarely talked about things. Emma had grown up in a Christian home with her mother, father, and two brothers. Their home was always quiet, calm, and well-kept. Whenever her parents disagreed about something, they didn't argue, but they also did not seem to work through their disagreement. Emma remembered a time when she was caught cheating on a test at school. The teacher wrote a note describing what Emma had done. Emma had to get her parents to sign the note. When Emma showed it to her parents at the dinner table, she held her breath, not knowing how they would react. After reading and signing the paper, her dad looked at her mother, then looked at Emma and grounded her for a week. He told her how disappointed he was in her. But not another word was said that night, nor in the days that followed. Without fail, after anything major would happen, her parents would acknowledge it but never ask any questions. Then nothing else was ever mentioned. It was like every experience, good or bad, slipped into a black hole.

Emma hasn't experienced overt evil like Joseph, but she also hasn't experienced overt comfort. After hearing about Steve's childhood, she had begun to see just how much she'd missed. It didn't seem fair.

Imbedded in this story is the same principle we find in Joseph's story. I like to call it the *50:20 principle*: Whenever we experience evil and injustice—whether overtly like Joseph or just through the typical inequalities of life like Emma—God still has a good purpose in view. This principle is showcased not only in Joseph's story but throughout the Bible. Let's look at Genesis 50:20 again in a little more detail.

The first part of the verse says, "As for you, you meant evil against me." It reminds us that people—not just Satan's forces—can seek to harm us and commit evil against us. We need to face the evil things done to us. We also need to understand how the sin committed against us can set off a domino effect within our souls. The evil we experience can distort the way we know and experience God, how we see ourselves, how we relate to others, and how we respond to life.

Now look at the second part of verse 20: "But God meant it for good, to bring it about that many people should be kept alive, as they are today." Truly knowing your story not only involves doing the difficult and intentional work of understanding how evil has impacted you. More importantly, it also involves seeing God at work in your story and knowing and experiencing his abiding love. God is at work in your story to bring about good from evil to accomplish his purposes.

He doesn't merely use our stories to keep people physically alive—as he kept people alive during the famine through Joseph's story—but he works to free us to live in Christ amidst the "powers of this dark world and against the spiritual forces of evil in the heavenly realms" (Ephesians 6:12). God speaks and acts so that we will know he is God and then respond with worship, praise, and trust in him alone.

Where Do You Start?

You may be warming up to the idea of looking, or looking again, at your story. But you may also feel anxious about doing something you have not done before, something that may prove difficult and tiring. No matter how you feel about it, I pray that the Spirit of God prompts you to keep your eyes on Jesus as you take this step of faith. Remember, Peter could walk on water as long as he kept his eyes on

Jesus; but the moment he was distracted by the wind and the waves, he sank.

You might wonder how to go about looking at your story.[3] Before you do anything else, pray and ask God to be with you and direct you. There are three steps involved:

The first step is to *remember*. Make a list of the life experiences that come to mind, whether or not they seem significant. Then arrange them in chronological order, grouping them in three broad categories: childhood, youth, and adulthood.

The second step is to *reflect*. Sort through the list of experiences and prayerfully consider how each experience has impacted how you see and understand yourself, others, and God. You can then see how these experiences have affected the way you relate to others and God. You will also look for *themes*, or big takeaway messages, from these experiences. Lastly, you will look for *patterns* of how you live and love that may have resulted from your life experiences.

The last step is to *recap*. At this point, connect the dots and write out your story. God tends to clarify our hearts and minds when we take the time to reflect and write out our thoughts, describe our life experiences, and express our desires.

The Beginning of Mark's Journey

After reaching a point of desperation about a lack of purpose and repeated disappointments in his life, Mark decided to take some time to look at his story. He wanted to discover some meaning in what seemed to be a meaningless life. In college, he took a history class in which his teacher suggested that history is not merely something you read about, but something you live. With this idea in mind, Mark decided to map out his history, starting from his childhood and youth into adulthood.

One of his earliest memories was wondering why he looked different from his brothers and sisters. Mark remembered his parents explaining to him that he is special because out of all the children they could have picked from an orphanage in South Korea, they chose him. This truth seemed less important the more he was teased by the kids in his schools or by his older brother, who would remind Mark that he was not and would never be his blood brother.

Reflecting on this particular aspect of his life drained Mark. He didn't realize how much his experiences growing up in a white family impacted how he saw the world around him. He also began to see a theme of *not belonging* emerge since his adoption. But that was just the beginning. Mark began to think deeply about why his biological parents gave him up for adoption. When he was younger, the consistent affirmation from his parents and the whirlwind of activities that kept the family busy didn't lend itself to such reflections. Plus, he was just a kid.

After spending a couple of hours listing the high and low points of his history and considering how these experiences had shaped him, Mark leaned back in his chair, closed his eyes, and thanked God for the tiring but helpful time of reflection. He didn't know it yet, but God was beginning a deep work in his life.

God's Invitation

Spend some time in God's Word. Open your heart to God about the parts of your story that leave you ashamed or fearful.

Read Psalm 23 slowly one or two times. As you receive his Word, listen to how God is speaking to the fear and shame related to your story. Your Good Shepherd has promised to lead you in his paths of righteousness as you journey through your story.

CHAPTER 3
KNOWING GOD
AND HIS REALITY
THROUGH HIS STORY

FOR NIKKI, love is elusive. She thought her parents loved each other, but they divorced. She struggled for years wondering if she could trust their love for her. After all, they failed to love each other. Mark felt loved growing up, but the more he thought about his biological parents, the more he questioned whether he was truly loved. Steve and Emma were confident about their love for one another in their dating and early married years; but as their years together went on and differences, conflicts, and challenges increased, they felt less convinced about love in general, and about their love for one another in particular.

We all long for love—we long to love and to be loved. And this doesn't apply only to people; we can love, even feel passion for, causes—for projects or movements that are important to us. We yearn to belong to a person or a group of people with whom we share love. We long to be known deeply and intimately. Such love for someone or something gives life meaning and purpose.

As we experience love and love others, three things seem to happen:

1. Love propels us towards the source or object of our love.
2. Love shifts our gaze away from ourselves and toward the one we love.
3. As we love another, love seems to grow within us.

When these things happen, we and our relationships flourish. All of these things are true about love . . . but there is one problem.

We Desire Love but Misunderstand It

If you could survey every person in the world and ask, "How do you define love? What do you expect out of love?" you'd get a wide variety of responses.

Some answers would reveal a *self-centered* perspective, a love based on what you perceive and experience. When we see love relationships portrayed in our culture, we hear statements like: "You make me feel special." "You understand me." "You make me feel important." "You serve me in such thoughtful and intentional ways." And don't forget the heartfelt, "You complete me."

Other survey responses would express an understanding of love primarily focused on warm and fuzzy feelings—a *feelings-centered* perspective. Feelings surge with a glance; there's love at first sight. "When I'm around you, I feel giddy"; or, "When I'm with you, I feel warm and safe." Unfortunately, such love can disappear in a flash or slowly dissipate like air from a tire with a slow leak—"The love is gone. I'm not feeling it anymore."

Some would view love from a *transactional* perspective. We all love in response to being loved. When we receive love, something stirs within us. "I love you because you treat me so well." Or, "I can't help but love you, given all you have done for me." This is well and good, but the reverse can also be true: sometimes we love to be loved. We might hear "I will shower her with gifts so that she will love me." Or, "The way to a man's heart is through his belly." There is an obvious downside to such manipulative, transactional love. We stop loving when we're not loved. It sounds like this: "I can never love you again, given what you did." Or, "You don't love me, why should I love you?"

Others will understand love from a *sacrificial* perspective, seeing it as the commitment to serve another regardless of their failures or the circumstances. Most wedding vows contain this sentiment. The thought that someone will love you "for better, for worse, for richer, for poorer, in sickness and in health," can move you to tears.

Each of these views captures elements of love. Each of these perspectives describe some truth about our experience of love, though some also reflect distorted understandings. But consider this: we will misunderstand love when we serve as our own frame of reference for love, that is, so long as our understanding of love is based on what we think, feel, and desire. When love is subjectively understood and experienced, we end up with a postmodern understanding: "What's true for you may not be true for me." But here is the irony, love is both subjective and objective.

If love is a universal reality, then it can be objectively known and experienced, no matter your gender, age, race, ethnicity, culture, or circumstance. In other words, what's true for you *is* also true for me. Given our unique personalities and stories, we do experience love in differing ways, but our experiences are bounded by a set spectrum of possibilities.

If love is objectively known and subjectively experienced, then what is the pathway to understanding it? We must look beyond ourselves to find the answer.

The Love That Surpasses Understanding

When we gaze upon beauty and grandeur, brilliance and majesty, something stirs within our souls and we are naturally drawn in. Whether it's an attractive person or the radiance of a vivid sunset, our hearts can flutter, leaving us speechless.

But if you experience a beautiful person as arrogant or rude, you will quickly change how you see them and feel about them. When a colorful sunset follows a tropical storm that flooded your home, you may not give it a second thought. In such cases, our subjective feelings are diminished by the objective reality.

But imagine a perfect love, a passionate affection, an overwhelming sense of awe, and an incomparable sense of beauty and majesty that never changes even amidst ever-changing circumstances. Imagine a love so perfect and pure that you would describe it as "better than life," and no one would call you a fool. Imagine a love that completely satisfies your every need and enables your soul to rest in total contentment. A perfect love that is always *present*. It pursues you all the days of your life whether you are awake or asleep. It is with you wherever you go, even to the heavens or to the depths of the ocean. Such love is with you and within you. This love serves as your refuge in fear, shame, loneliness, and sorrow.

Imagine a lover who *promises* never to leave you or forsake you—and then keeps his promises. His love is always faithful; his every spoken word can be trusted and will always come true. And this lover is *powerful*. He provides above and beyond all that you can ask or imagine, and he protects you from all fear as you travel through the valleys of darkness.

Imagine a perfect, present, promised, and powerful love. Wouldn't it *reframe* how you see and experience life? Picture a love that *restores* the brokenness in your soul and can wipe away every tear and painful memory. Consider a love that can defeat death. Such love *redeems* every unwanted and hurtful part of your story and ushers you into paradise. Such incomparable love would embrace and stir your heart and soul forever.

Where is such love found? Does it even exist? You've probably heard it said, "Love makes the world go 'round." Another way of saying this is, "Love is the principal force behind human life. In medieval theology, it was held that love literally set the universe in motion."[4] If the saying is right, such love can't be discovered through the wisdom or strength of humans, but only through divine revelation.

Love Is Divine

Before creation, perfect love existed and was experienced. How do we know this to be true? Because God is love (1 John 4:8, 16). God existed eternally as Father, Son, and Holy Spirit, even before creating the universe (Genesis 1:1–2; John 17:5). When Jesus was with his disciples, he prayed to his heavenly Father, saying, "You loved me before the creation of the world" (John 17:24). Imagine the Holy

Trinity enjoying perfect love that flowed equally and infinitely from each person. Consider the joy, peace, pleasure, and affection that each member experienced within their being. Such love was and is glorious.

Let's consider two important implications of the reality that God is love:

1. Since God is love, none of his actions can ever be considered to be unloving. Even his holiness, sovereignty, and wrath are compatible with his love. This is hard for us to accept. Think about how often you may question God's love when something bad happens or when something you hoped for doesn't come about.
2. God's love is consistent and orderly. It always flows from the Father to the Son by his Spirit. This progression counters our temptation to see God the Father as unloving and wrathful while viewing Jesus as loving.

Nikki saw God as unloving and absent, given the way her father became a different person after her parents' divorce. Emma also wrestled with these truths. She grew up seeing God the Father as an angry, judgmental, hard-to-please God who expected her to be perfect and would punish her when she was not. Her pastor would scream and yell as he preached about God's wrath against and punishment for those who didn't live right. He used guilt as a tactic to make people trust and obey God. Both of these women should sit back and ponder the reality that God *is* love.

Consider this beautiful truth: The love you long for *does* exist and can be experienced apart from your circumstances.

Knowing love originates with God offers hope and changes everything. How so? Even if your father or mother never expressed their love to you, love can be found. You can taste love and find satisfaction in God. Though you may feel un-lovable, you can be confident that you are loved, because Love gave himself for you. And because you've received love, you can also give love to others. For example, you can love your spouse even when feelings aren't there. Even if your story has left you skeptical, you can love and forgive your enemies.

It may be that you're pushing back on the reality that God is love. It doesn't seem to correspond with what you've experienced in your story. But his love is inviting you to shift your eyes away from your story. He wants you to shift your gaze and see his story as your frame of reference.

God's Story of Love

It can be hard for us to comprehend how love begins and ends with God. But love is a major theme of God's true story. Let's take a look at how it is tied to the four acts of God's story:

1. *At creation, we see how God created us for love.* What's re-markable about the beginning of God's story, as revealed in the Bible, is that God created every person to experience the same love the Father, Son, and Spirit have eternally enjoyed. God not only created every woman, man, girl, and boy to know and experience his love, but he also created us to love him with our entire being. He made us for an intimate relationship with him. We see this love relationship in the first great love command:

"Love the Lord your God with all your heart and with all your soul and with all your mind" (Matthew 22:37). God also created us to love others so they might know and experience his love. Jesus shows us this with the second love command: "Love your neighbor as yourself" (Matthew 22:39).

2. *The fall shows us how evil keeps us from love.* As we saw earlier, evil infiltrated the first man and woman as soon as they disobeyed God. Our holy God will not dwell with those who desire to know and do evil; it would not be loving. So, our first parents' evil desires and deeds broke their intimate relationship with Love himself. Since their fall, every subsequent generation has been born sinful. Sin and evil have distorted God's design for love. They keep us from knowing God and his love, and they misdirect our love so that we love ourselves first and foremost instead of loving God and others. Such misdirected love is the reason why relationships are hard and hurtful.

3. *Redemption shows us how Jesus restores us with love.* God knew we were no match for evil. When we try to live in our own strength, sin always overpowers and enslaves us. In the definitive moment of God's story, Love came down from heaven to earth to rescue us from our incurable condition. He did this in a way the wise thought foolish and the strong ridiculed. John, who was Jesus's beloved disciple, described God's perfect and powerful love: "This is how God showed his love among us: He sent his one and only Son into the world that we might live through him. This is love: not that we loved God, but that he loved us and sent his Son as an atoning sacrifice for our sins" (1 John 4:9–10). Not only did God's love in

Christ come down from heaven but Jesus lived a sinless life, died the death we deserved, conquered sin and death, and then rose from the dead. Then, God the Father did one more incredible thing to untwist our distorted love. He poured out his love into our hearts through his Spirit so that, having been saved in Christ, we might now be able to love God and others (Romans 5:5).

4. *Consummation shows us how we will enjoy love forever.* Even as Christians, we still struggle with loving God and others. This is because we are still living in the time of the fall where evil seeks to keep us from love. But here is good news: Even though we are still living in a broken world, we are now living in Christ, and his Spirit of love dwells in us. At the end of God's story, the consummation, we will enjoy love forever. When God destroys evil in the new heavens and earth, we will freely and fully love God and others in ways that will make the best romance story pale in comparison.

In his story, God brings us into his covenant of love, wherein he loves us with an everlasting love. In this true love story, God ensures that nothing can or will ever separate us from his love. He desires us to abide in his love forever and live with him and for him. But here is more good news: we do not have to wait for heaven to enjoy such love. We can enjoy God's perfect love now, in the present—even at this very moment.

God's Story Gives Understanding to Your Story

Maybe you are still tempted to dismiss what you've read given everything you have been through in life. Perhaps you are weary and have grown cynical toward God, believing he doesn't care about you. Others of you may believe that God is love, but you have been in a dry season for longer than you can remember. You may have forgotten what it is like to know and experience God's love, and his story seems like a mirage in the desert. Still others of you may be in another place. Your heart adores God when you worship him on Sundays, but the rest of the week, he seems far away, and you can't understand why.

Let's take a look at a diagram that may put your reality into perspective.

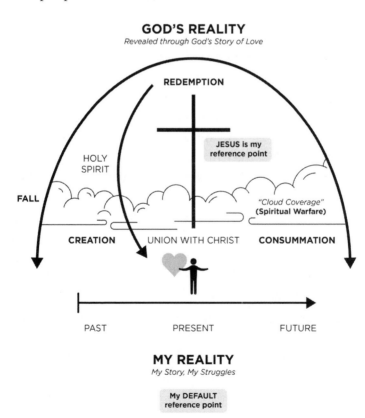

45

At the bottom of the diagram is a person with a past, present, and future time line. This represents *your reality*, made up of your story and struggles. Of course, life is not only about difficulties, but the hardships and pain of life tend to shape how we see and understand it. Often our life experiences—both good and bad—serve as our primary reference point. We frame and filter everything through what we have known and experienced.

For Emma, her reference points were exposed in her conflicts with her husband. She and Steve seemed to fight constantly. Steve would want to talk things through immediately, but Emma would just shut down and not share anything. Growing up, Steve and his mom would talk about anything, anytime. But Emma's family rarely talked about anything meaningful, especially after an argument. So, when they married, Steve and Emma had opposing ideas on how to relate to one another after an argument. They had different reference points from their personal stories.

Now, look at the entire diagram. You will see that your reality is a part of God's bigger and more glorious reality. We must not look only to the reference points we have in this life, but interpret our story through God's overarching story. God's reality showcases his story of love revealed through the four major acts: *creation, fall, redemption*, and *consummation*.

Cloud coverage across the middle of the diagram represents *spiritual warfare*, the efforts of Satan's forces to keep us from knowing and experiencing God. Imagine being at the airport during a thunderstorm. Even though it may be daytime, you can't see the sun because of the gray clouds spread across the sky. But as soon as your plane takes off and punches through the clouds, the sun appears in all its brilliance as you leave the storm clouds below. Seeing both the sun and the clouds should remind us that two realities can coexist. Emma and Steve were stuck under the clouds, living as if they were not in God's story. Even though you may live in the dark and painful realities of the fall, you are also living in God's loving and beautiful world.

At the center of the diagram, *redemption* is illustrated by the cross, which spans from high in the heavens and penetrates deep down below the clouds. Jesus came from heaven into our fallen world. Through his life, death, and resurrection, he made it possible for us to have life *with* God, that is, life in *union with Christ*. God also poured out his love into our hearts through his Holy Spirit, illustrated by the arrow toward the heart. The indwelling Spirit makes our union with Christ a powerful, life-giving reality.

Because we are united with Christ, Jesus becomes our new reference point, instead of our past, present, and future experiences. Jesus, who is always faithful, true, and good, serves as the frame and filter for our experiences.

What does it mean practically for Jesus to be your reference point? Think about those times when you feel alone. Perhaps you live by yourself, or even when people surround you, you feel like no one knows you or cares about you. From the standpoint of your experience, this may be true—both objectively and subjectively. But as one who is in union with Christ, you are never alone, and you are more loved than you could imagine.

Let's consider another example. You may struggle to forgive someone who has been rude to you at work. From your perspective, you may think you have every right to be rude in return. But when you make Jesus your reference point, you see that he calls you to forgive those who offend you; and he calls you to love them, knowing that he forgave and loved you even when you were his enemy.

Looking back at the diagram, you will see that the labels for *creation* and *consummation* are below the clouds. This reminds us there once was a time when there was no cloud coverage—humanity walked with God in the garden. Moreover, there is coming a day when we will live without the cloud coverage again. In the new heavens and earth, our stories and God's story will be seamless, and we will enjoy his perfect love and presence without end. As we live on this side of heaven, God's creation and consummation realities serve as "guardrails" to remind us who we are and inform us how God calls us to live in a confusing, fallen world.

A Story to Be Lived

If you are like most people, those future blessings of the consummation seem too far away to help you at the moment. Your present pain and anxiety draw your heart and mind inward. Your body responds with shallow breathing, tense shoulders, and an aching stomach. Something has to break through the clouds to pull your eyes upward to remind you of God's bigger reality.

Mark pulled out a book he had read in college that taught him about God's story being the framework for understanding God's Word. The book said that Jesus was the central point of this grand narrative. An idea came to him as he skimmed through his yellow highlights and read his scribbled notes in the margins. Mark wondered if God's story could somehow help him to better understand his own story. He felt hopeful and fearful at the same time. Hopeful because he had been longing for a sense of meaning and purpose. Fearful because he was unsure of what he would discover as he embarked on this journey. His biggest fear was that God's story would not offer him any direction or insight about his life.

A great movie or a well-written novel can transport you into a different reality where you can live vicariously through the characters as they encounter danger or fall in love. As good as a great story is at helping you experience a different reality for a moment, the sobering truth is that after the movie or book comes to an end, your reality comes crashing back again. You do not have the option of living in someone else's story.

However, God's story offers far more than you could ever think or imagine.

First, God's story includes your story. Amazingly, he chose you before he created the world. He formed you in your mother's womb. Before you were even born, God knew every twist and turn of your life. He sees and understands every thought, emotion, and desire you ever had and will ever have. He is aware of every hurt and disappointment and every way your heart longs for love.

Second, when you die, your story will still be intimately connected with his story. You will be overwhelmed by his glory and free to enjoy God's love, joy, and peace in unimaginable ways. Now you may dismiss his prior knowledge as the past and his future realities as too far away. But the final incomparable truth is that God invites you to live in his story now, in the present. No movie or book comes close to such an invitation!

Now that you have taken time to consider how your story shapes you and how God invites you into his bigger story, it's time to journey through his story.

God's Invitation

Spend some time in God's Word. Open your heart to God about the parts of his story that stir your imagination and give you hope. You can be honest with him if you are struggling to understand how his story will make a difference in your reality.

Read Psalm 25 slowly once or twice as you keep in mind what you shared with God. God calls you to trust him in your doubts and confusion.

CHAPTER 4
CREATION: GOD CREATED US FOR LOVE

CAN YOU imagine being an observer when God created the heavens and earth? The biggest IMAX theater and longest National Geographic documentary would not come close to capturing such majestic and mind-blowing realities.

First, consider that God created the universe from nothing. Then recognize that he didn't create a reality with a simplistic design, small dimensions, or monochrome colors. With his limitless imagination, God brought our complex, expansive, and beautiful universe into existence. He produced somewhere between five million and one trillion species of life on earth. He also created the human body, with its thirty trillion cells that work in harmony. The expanse of God's world stretches to the outer limits of one hundred billion ever-expanding galaxies, over thirteen billion light-years away.[5] And the beauty of his created works can't be fully captured by the ten million shades of color that the human eye can perceive.[6] When you consider the fact that God made such vastness from nothing, simply by his word, can you better understand how it is only he who can appoint the times and boundaries of nations (Acts 17:26)? Can you see more tangibly how he can move the mountains in your life as well?

God spoke, and life began. What God desires, he makes happen. God's creative word is powerful.

God's Word Reveals His Loving Care

We view the terms *Bible* and *God's Word* as nearly synonymous—but we can reduce them. Unfortunately, we sometimes think of God's Word as merely ink on pages, as words originally written thousands of years ago, rather than seeing them as equally powerful to the Word God used to create everything. We can fall into the trap of seeing the Bible as something we are supposed to read to be a good Christian or something we read so that our day goes better, but this reduces the reality of God's Word to a guilt-driven obligation. It becomes a moral guide with good stories, or in the worst case, an irrelevant book that doesn't address the realities of life.

Imagine an advertisement about a product that has millions of likes. This product makes its claims in capital letters, not fine print. It promises to give you joy, bring delight to your heart, preserve your life, strengthen your weary soul, keep you from being deceived, broaden your understanding about life and relationships, and enable you to experience unfailing love. It offers commitments guaranteed to come true, it gives hope to your fainting soul, it empowers you to walk in freedom, it comforts you in your suffering, it keeps you from perishing in your affliction, it prevents you from being put to shame, stays with you always, makes you wiser than your enemies, gives you more insight than all of your teachers, keeps you from every evil path, serves as the joy of your heart, sustains and upholds you so that you are never hopeless, and directs your footsteps so that no sin will rule over you. It can be fully trusted because its thoroughly tested. It refreshes your soul, makes wise the simple, gives joy to your heart, is more precious than gold, tastes sweeter than honey, and allows you to hear God's voice and know his heart. Even in this commercial age, you can get this product for free at certain locations around the world, but you can also find free access to a virtual version of it twenty-four seven on the internet.

It sounds too good to be true. Can any product offer such unbelievable results? Yet in Psalms 19 and 119, God makes all of these claims about his Word, to not only reveal his heart, but so that we can know and experience his love.

If you sit back and think about your previous experience with God's Word, you might be initially skeptical about the Bible's incredible claims. But if you accept by faith that God created everything in the heavens and on earth through his spoken word, then can't you also accept that God will, through his Word, make these promises a reality for every one of his children? You don't have to be a pastor or theologian to experience God's life-giving Word. You don't have to sit on a mountaintop or go on a multiday retreat to hear God's voice and know his heart. You can hide his Word in your heart and meditate on it day and night.

God uses his Word to show his love for us. The primary ways God loved and cared for the first man and woman in the garden was through his life-giving presence and words. Sure, he provided for their practical needs, but what their souls needed came through their intimate relationship with

God, through hearing and following his Word. Imagine, God designed his spoken Word to be received and lived out as the means of life with him. Even now, the reality of God's life-giving Word is guaranteed through his Spirit and promised through Jesus Christ. Through it, he shows us his love today.

But if this is true, why do we struggle to experience such benefits from God's Word? There's no one answer, but multiple reasons. In short, we can struggle to know and experience God's Word in these ways when we fail to read it; or when we read it but don't slow down to reflect on its truths and allow it to stir our imaginations and affections. Doubts and disobedience also keep God and his Word at a distance, and the enemy seeks to undermine God's Word and cause us to doubt God's love. Our trials and troubles can also prompt us to question God and his goodness, sometimes to the point where we turn our backs on him and his Word.

In college, one of Nikki's best friends invited her to a Bible study. Within months, Nikki came to see her need for Christ, and she gave her life to him. But now she's graduated from college and jumped into the workforce. She doesn't remember the last time she opened her Bible. And if Nikki does remind herself to spend time with God before she dashes off to work, she doesn't get much out of reading her Bible, because she finds herself distracted with what she has to do that day.

Steve has been preoccupied with Bella, his coworker. Being around her seems to have sparked new life in him, and this has led to increasing doubts about God and his marriage. On Sundays during the worship service, Steve goes through the motions of singing, praying, and listening to the sermon.

At first, Steve's doubts about God alarmed him because he had experienced such intimate times with God through high school, college, and during his first few years of marriage. But recently, Steve has accepted his doubts as a way of life; God seems more distant and increasingly irrelevant.

Whatever your obstacles to knowing and experiencing God through his Word, he wants you to remember that experiencing his presence through his living Word provides what your body and soul need. When you understand that Jesus is the Word of God, you will begin to see that God's Word is your only hope (John 1:1; Revelation 19:13). God's Word is the green pasture and still waters that he uses to restore your weary and broken soul (Psalm 23).

God Created You for Communion with Love

Take a moment to imagine the Father, Son, and Holy Spirit at the second they decided to create you. In this decisive moment, they made you with joy and delight, with purpose and a plan.

This became real to Mark when he read Psalm 139 during his morning commute. He found himself reflecting on the profound realities of God's intentional work, forming him in his mother's womb, breathing life into him, and knowing every day of his existence before he came into this world (Psalm 139:13–16). He was so preoccupied with these truths as he stared out the train window that he almost missed his stop.

As he reflected on how God wanted him to be born—though his biological parents did not keep him—he was comforted. Mark considered how God knew about his days before he was born. God knew when he was all alone in the orphanage. God knew when his adoptive parents prayed for months for a baby to adopt, and how they raised money for his adoption. And God even knew when kids bullied him at school and left him with broken bones. God also knew that now he struggled with loneliness and a lack of purpose. The reality that God knew all his days and formed him intentionally and purposefully encouraged Mark. God, in his bigger story, knew every part of Mark's. He was excited to see how God's story connected with his own, and his curiosity skyrocketed as he imagined what plans God still had for his future.

Believe it or not, God created you to know and experience his love, the same love that eternally existed between the Father, Son, and Holy Spirit. That love is God's story for you. How can we experience such love? It's all in his divine design.

God created you for communion with him, to enjoy the intimate and everlasting love of the Trinity. Communion with God describes how we experience our relationship with him. Take a moment to consider this incredible reality: the God of the universe invites you into the communion *of* God through your communion *with* God. In other words, God doesn't invite you to enjoy a second-rate version of fellowship with him. Instead, he gives you the privilege of joining the real deal, the actual communion of the Father, Son, and Holy Spirit.

In the old days, you risked your life if you entered into a king's presence without permission. The king needed to invite you to come into his courts. Similarly, the Israelites were not allowed to set foot on Mount Sinai, where God met with Moses, or else they would be put to death

(Exodus 19:12). Even on the Day of Atonement, only the high priest could enter into the Holy of Holies, the inner court where God's presence dwelt. The Old Testament restrictions about drawing near to God show us how our sinfulness keeps us from entering into his holy presence.

At the cross God solved the problem of our separation from his presence. Jesus's death paid the penalty for our sins. His resurrection and ascension make our communion with God possible as we live in Christ. God's story enables us to enjoy communion with him as we live in this broken world. Communion with God involves three aspects: knowing, experiencing, and imaging God.

Knowing God

It's hard to wrap your mind around the reality that the Creator of the heavens and earth not only made you, but wants you to know him—God created you to know him. The verb "to know" in the Hebrew conveys knowing someone intimately as a husband and wife know one another deeply and fully. God doesn't merely want you to know *about* him, or even to be *acquainted with* him. God wants you to know the depths of his heart and to understand his life-giving words.

John wrote, "Now this is eternal life: that they know you, the only true God" (John 17:3).

In other words, life is knowing God, who both gives you life and sustains and renews your life. Eternal life is knowing and living with your eternal God. As Christians, this means we can enjoy eternal life now, rather than wait until we die and go to heaven.

The reality that she is known by and can know God has changed Nikki's perspective. Nikki had struggled for years with a longing to be known and to know others deeply. As a result of her hectic life, she has feared growing old without having anyone to share her hopes and struggles. She would wonder, *Will anyone truly know me? Will anyone notice when I die?* In her attempt to alter the course of her career-driven life, she decided to accept an invitation from one of her coworkers to attend church on Sunday. When she went, her heart was captivated by something the pastor preached from John 17:3. Nikki realized that she had been so focused on being known that she had never thought about God wanting her to know him. This shift in perspective changed her in ways that were hard to explain. As God reminded her that he already knew her better than anyone else could know her, her longing to be known was relieved. She found herself taking a deep breath, and her body relaxed as she reflected on this mutual relationship. Nikki discovered that she is already known, desired, and loved, and in this relationship, God has invited her to know, desire, and love him.

Experiencing God

God also created you to experience him in deeply personal ways through your body and soul. God made you so that you can experience his beauty and love through what you see, smell, hear, taste, and touch. Emma felt closest to God when she would take long walks outdoors. She would smell the sweet scent of honeysuckles, hear the gentle flow of the creek meandering through the woods, and see the sunlight piercing through the dense forest where deer leisurely fed on plants. Emma would talk to God as she marveled at his creation.

In his wisdom, God connected your soul and body seamlessly so that what impacts one part of you impacts all of you. Whatever stresses your soul also stresses your body. Regardless of whether your stress comes from an approaching deadline, screaming kids, a difficult marriage, or a relentless work schedule, life's stressful demands can have many physical effects. Stress can raise your blood pressure, increase the cortisol in your bloodstream, disrupt your digestive system, cause headaches, etc. Conversely, whatever impacts your body also impacts your soul. Whenever you get a cold, you can also lose motivation to do work or become short-tempered because you don't feel well.

When Steve and Emma first fell in love, their hearts stirred with a deep affection for one another. It gave each of them a renewed sense of meaning and purpose. They experienced boundless energy as they enjoyed hours of conversations, making the most of their time together. They would agree that love does something special for your body and soul.

Remember that God is love. He created us in such a way that we are most impacted by love in general, and by his love in particular. King David described the unique nature of God's love when he proclaimed that it is better than life. Such love fully satisfied him "as with the richest of foods" (Psalm 63:3–5). God knows we need tangible realities to understand the realities of his love. There is hardly a person alive who doesn't groan with delight or close their eyes with a satisfied smile as they enjoy a bite of their favorite food. If we enjoy delicious food with wholehearted and whole-body responses, it makes sense that God created us to enjoy his love in even greater ways, to the point where we declare with King David, "Lord, your love is better than life." God's love is the only thing that satisfies us, the only thing that brings ultimate contentment to our souls.

The apostle Paul personally testified to a second, unique role of God's love in our lives when he wrote, "For Christ's love compels us . . . that those who live should no longer live for themselves but for him who died for them and was raised again" (2 Corinthians 5:14–15). In other words, God's love is the only thing powerful enough to compel us to live for him. To *compel* means to urge or motivate strongly. When you feel compelled, you just can't help yourself. God created us to be compelled or controlled by his love in such a way that we live for him instead of living for ourselves.

Imaging God

If you are struggling to feel affection for God, if you lack satisfaction and are feeling discontent, if you are dry when you read his Word, it may feel like God is distant and that what you do doesn't matter. When we don't know God intimately and struggle to experience his love in our whole being, it makes sense that we will also be uninterested in—or perhaps feel that it's impossible to try—following him. But how we live matters to God. It's part of our communion with him.

When Paul teaches the philosophers at Mars Hill about their unknown God, he describes God as the one who made heaven and earth, who is not served by human hands, who gives everyone life and breath and establishes the times and boundaries of all nations. He concludes by saying, "For in him we live and move and have our being" (Acts 17:28). Paul teaches that God created us in such a way that in him we live and move and exist, and every aspect of who we are should be informed by God, who created us in his image

(Genesis 1:26–27). Being created in God's image means that he created us to reflect him as we relate and respond to him and others. He wants us to display his righteousness as it is revealed in his Word.

Being made in God's image means that he designed every aspect of our lives to be informed by his will, his ways, and his wise shepherding. God knew we needed a tangible example to understand what it means to be formed in his image, so he sent Jesus, who serves as the best example since he is the perfect image of God (Colossians 1:15; Hebrews 1:3). *Practically speaking, being made in God's image means he created us to live and love like Jesus.*

Why Communion with God Matters

Mark was overwhelmed when he pondered the realities of his communion with God. He realized that he could actually commune with the God of the universe during his commute to and from work. This transformed his forty-five-minute ride with a train car full of strangers into an intimate time with God, one that was filled with reading and reflecting on God's Word. But when Mark reflected on how he was created to *know* God, this also helped to ease his pain of not being wanted by his biological parents.

The incredible idea that God wanted Mark to *experience* his eternal love also enabled him to have a better understanding of God's purpose for his emotions, which he tends to suppress. Emotions give depth and color to life, helping us to more fully know and experience our relationships with God and others. Emotions also help to make truths about God come alive (Psalm 34:8; 63:1–8). As Mark thought about how God created him in his image, he began to see how God wanted him to live wholeheartedly for him. God was counteracting Mark's struggles with loneliness and purposelessness through the Spirit-empowered connections he was discovering between his story and God's.

These three aspects of our communion with God play a crucial role in how we live. Knowing God enables us to live *with* him. Experiencing God compels us to live *for* him. Imaging God results as we live *like* him. Such a life not only gives purpose but also provides direction for how we should live and love.

God's Invitation

Spend some time in God's Word. Open your heart to God and share with him how you have been experiencing your relationship with him. Do you sense that God knows you intimately, or does he seem distant? When was the last time you experienced his love for you?

Read Psalm 139 slowly once or twice as you keep in mind what you shared with God. How does this passage help you to know and experience your God?

CHAPTER 5
CREATION: JESUS IS OVER ALL CREATION

EMMA SENSED something had shifted in her marriage. Steve seemed distracted and sometimes disinterested as they spent time together in the evenings and on weekends. She felt he was pulling away from her. She asked him a few times if there was anything wrong or if there was something between them. He would simply respond, "Everything is fine." But she knew things were not okay with him or between them. After several weeks of this unusual interaction, Emma found herself crying herself to sleep many nights.

Weeks later, Steve came home late from work, and Emma's suspicions solidified when he hugged her. She caught a whiff of perfume on him that she didn't recognize, and it prompted her to confront him about the great fear which had been keeping her up all hours of the night.

In a calm but firm tone, Emma asked Steve, "Are you seeing another woman?" He immediately fired back, "Of course not! Are you crazy? Why would you even think that?" Emma proceeded to share her recent observations—his growing distance and his lack of interest in her as his wife or in their relationship as a couple. She also pointed out that he'd been working late with increasing regularity, and that, on a couple of occasions, she had tried to verify his whereabouts, but no one in the office could locate him.

Steve continued to deny any wrongdoing. Then, Emma dropped a copy of their phone records on the kitchen table and ramped up her volume as she pointed to a highlighted number that showed up repeatedly after work and on weekends. Steve again denied there was another woman until Emma picked up her phone to call the number. Steve screamed, "What are you doing?" and grabbed the phone out of her hand. He'd been found out. Emma broke down sobbing.

In the days and weeks that followed, Emma found herself preoccupied with why the affair had happened. *How could Steve ruin our marriage? What could I have done differently?* Emma also found herself questioning God. *Why would you let this happen? What good could you ever bring about from this mess? I thought you loved me!*

Such questions easily flow from our hearts when we're hurting and confused. Heartache draws us inward as we seek answers, and it directs our eyes outward as we look for *something* or *someone* to blame. If we look up, we can find ourselves doubting God's goodness. Remember, we were not created to know or experience evil. But when we do, our world can spin out of control, and we can start feeling hopeless.

Believe it or not, the realities we learn through the story of creation serve to guide and anchor us during the storms of life. It's easy to dismiss the truth that God created us to have loving communion with him when our realities are pressing, painful, and persistent. God's promise of loving communion can seem pointless, especially when our circumstances serve as cloud cover that blinds us from seeing the bigger reality of God's story. Amid our questions and confusion, knowing God can be an afterthought. Experiencing God's love, joy, and peace can seem like a cruel mirage in the desert. In the midst of brokenness, the thoughts, emotions, and desires that flood our souls can override any motivation to live the kind of life that images God.

You may feel the urge to do whatever it takes to relieve the pain, get even, or pull away from everyone. But God has known every day of your life from before you were born. He knows your troubles, your pain, and the times you've cried for help. In spite of the difficulty, God invites you to draw near to him for refuge and rest.

God also knows how evil has distorted the way you see and understand life—even how it has distorted your view of him. God understands how evil has damaged your soul, broken you down, and drained your will to live. God is familiar with the ways evil seeks to be the center and defining theme of your story—the ways it shapes how you see yourself and your life. He knows that you can't fight evil in your own strength. And he wants you to know that Jesus makes a difference.

In Him: The Backstory on Jesus and Creation

If we have a simplistic understanding of God's story, we won't see Christ in God's work of creation and what that reality means for us. Many of us think God the Son first interacted with creation when he came from heaven to earth as a baby in the Bethlehem manger. But if we look further, we will see that the Son brought all of creation into existence.

> The Son is the image of the invisible God, the first-born over all creation. For *in him* all things were created: things in heaven and on earth, visible and invisible, whether thrones or powers or rulers or authorities; all things have been created *through him* **and** *for him.* He is before all things, and *in him all things hold together.* And he is the head of the body, the church; he is the beginning and the firstborn from among the dead, so that **in everything he might have the supremacy**. For God was pleased to have *all his fullness dwell in him,* and *through him to reconcile to himself all things,* whether things on earth or things in heaven, by making peace through his blood, shed on the cross. (Colossians 1:15–20, emphasis mine)

The world often refers to creation as Mother Nature, but all creation was actually made in, through, and for the Son. Nothing in creation was made apart from Christ, the Word. The apostle John confirms what we've read from Paul when he writes, "In the beginning was the Word, and the Word was with God, and the Word was God. He was with God in the beginning. Through him all things were made; without him nothing was made that has been made" (John 1:1–3). Creation has never existed without him.

Why is it so important for us to see that Jesus Christ is over all of creation? Because God wants us to see his glory in the face of Christ. And he wants us to see that this glory stretches from the beginning to the end of God's story (2 Corinthians 4:6).

Jesus is not only majestic, but his glory changes us when we set our eyes on him. But it's not until we see the glory of Christ, that we will shift our gaze from our fears and confusion to him.

Jesus is not only powerful, but he became weak so that we can have life in him. But it's not until we see the power of Christ in weakness, that we will draw near to him for refuge in our own weakness.

Jesus not only created us, but he knows what we need and how to care for us. But it's not until we understand the intimate knowledge and intentional care with which he created us, that we will look to him as our Good Shepherd.

In these and many other ways, Jesus serves as our reference point. He helps us understand who we are and how we should live in this hard and hurtful world.

Through Him: Jesus Is Your Reference Point

As we saw in chapter 2, our tendency is to see and understand life through the lens of our own experiences. In one sense, this is part of God's design. He made us so that we can relate to new events and experiences with what we already know as a point of reference. That's simply part of how we learn and grow.

Similarly, throughout the Scriptures, God calls his people to remember who he is and the marvelous works he has done so they can live with confidence, clinging to his goodness and faithfulness. Who God is, what he has done for us, and what he promises to do should be our ultimate frame of reference—our big-picture reference point.

Sadly, with the fall, evil skewed our frame of reference. It changed the way we understand life by shifting our primary reference point from God to ourselves. Since the fall, our human stories have been framed primarily by our painful experiences and chronic struggles; we live with tunnel vision.

When we consider creation, we're reminded that God made us to "live, move, and have our being" in him (Acts 17:28). As Jesus told his disciples, "I am the way and the truth and the life" (John 14:6). From these two passages, we see that God designed us so that Jesus is our reference point for every aspect of life. Christ is our North Star, our never-changing indicator, who helps us know where we are and where we need to go (Malachi 3:6; James 1:17).

Jesus tells us what happens when we seek to live life without him as our reference point, the grid through which we understand and approach each day. He said, "I am the vine; you are the branches. If you remain in me and I in you, you will bear much fruit; apart from me you can do nothing" (John 15:5). If you do not make Jesus your reference point, you will never make sense of your reality. You'll remain perplexed with regard to who you are and how you are to live. You will be confused about God so long as you fail to trust him and his promises. You will also struggle to experience his love, and you'll lack the desire and ability to live for him and like him in your circumstances. But when you make God's story your point of reference, it will transform how you experience him and your life. When we live *through* Jesus, things change.

As Nikki spent more time with Jesus, something happened. As she learned to abide in Christ through his Word, she learned more about God's heart, became more familiar with his words and ways, and experienced his love and comfort more regularly and personally. She noticed a shift in her perspective, and she began to see and experience life differently even though her circumstances had not changed. As Nikki spent more time reflecting on God's love and faithfulness, she thought and talked less about her parents' divorce. She also noticed that as she shared with others what God was teaching her, he was changing her attitude and how she viewed life. She enjoyed learning about how Jesus lived, knowing that he experienced more trials and troubles than she could ever experience, yet without sin. She marveled at Jesus's ability to submit to and follow his Father's will in spite of the adversity he faced. She was humbled by the realization that Jesus's obedience was for her sake. Nikki now experienced greater contentment and was more at peace whether in the grind of work or in the silence of her days off; Jesus was becoming her never-changing reference point.

For Him: Jesus Is Your Purpose

Colossians 1 not only says that all things were created *in Christ* and *through Christ*. It also says that creation was accomplished *for Christ*. Jesus is the goal of all creation. Everything exists for him—for his pleasure, joy, and glory. All creation was made to testify to him: "The heavens declare the glory of God; the skies proclaim the work of his hands. Day after day they pour forth speech; night after night they reveal knowledge. They have no speech, they use no words; no sound is heard from them. Yet their voice goes out into all the earth, their words to the ends of the world" (Psalm 19:1–4).

Take a moment to reflect on what it means for you, as a human being made in God's image, that all creation testifies to Christ's goodness and glory. People are the crowning jewels of God's creation, and we are made for Christ. What does that mean for how you understand your purpose in life? How does that inform the way you should live?

We live in a visible world, but we must remember that it was made with an invisible purpose. The universe was made for more than we can see. All things, including us, were made for Jesus. We were made to live for him—for his pleasure, purposes, and praise—and not for ourselves.

Over the years, Mark struggled with his purpose in life. He was confused because it seemed that a person's purpose centered around what they do for a living. When he was young, people would ask him, "What do you want to do when you grow up?" When he got to college, the main question he'd hear was, "What is your major?" These days, whenever he meets someone, the first question seems to be, "What do you do?" These common questions combined to shape how he understands his purpose in life.

Mark had a good job as a computer analyst. He enjoyed what he did, and he was good at it. But he'd never dreamed about this career as a kid, and he struggled with whether or not he would be content in this line of work for the rest of his life. Though he had a good job and a promising career, Mark sensed there had to be more to life than work, video games, mountain biking, and hanging out with friends.

During his commute home one day, he read Paul's reflection on his own life before Christ: "But whatever were gains to me I now consider loss for the sake of Christ. What is more, I consider everything a loss because of the surpassing worth of knowing Christ Jesus my Lord, for whose sake I have lost all things. I consider them garbage, that I may gain Christ and be found in him" (Philippians 3:7–9). Mark paused and stared out the window; Paul's words shattered his cultural understanding of one's life purpose.

In Philippians 3, Paul outlines his impressive family lineage, education, and accomplishments. Then the apostle writes that he considers all these things to be rubbish when compared to knowing Christ and being found in him. Mark continued to read how Paul wanted to know Christ and become like him through his life, suffering, and death. As he read, questions flooded Mark's mind and heart. *Is this why God made me? Is my overarching goal in life to know Christ and live in a way that brings him glory? Will working as a computer analyst, or being a husband or father, satisfy the deep longing in my soul for a purpose that is bigger than myself?* It dawned on Mark that maybe he was looking for ultimate fulfillment in the wrong places.

In a practical yet profound way, Jesus summarizes our overarching purpose in life with two simple commands: Love God with your entire being and love others as he has loved you (Matthew 22:37–39; John 13:34). Loving God with our whole life means that we live with and for him so that we can live like him. Jesus again states it simply in John 14:15, "If you love me, keep my commands." This grand purpose—loving God and others—should inform all the other secondary purposes in our lives whether they be associated with our vocation, our relationships, or our social activism.

God's purpose in creating you for Christ informs your purpose for living. He made you to experience and enjoy his love so that you can love him and others. *God's divine purpose is what ultimately satisfies you and brings him glory.* Such purpose extends far beyond your own life and brings a peace to the depths of your soul. Moreover, this purpose reframes and redeems a life story marked by suffering, struggles, and injustice.

Jesus Holds All Things Together

The earth revolves around the sun at roughly sixty-six thousand miles per hour. What keeps it from moving out of its orbit? The human heart beats more than 2.5 billion times over an average lifespan. What keeps it going? We take these functional realities for granted. But Colossians 1:17 tells us that Jesus holds all things together. He holds the laws of gravity and physics and the life force behind all of our biological processes. They are all sustained by his "powerful word" (Hebrews 1:3). If Jesus ceased his sustaining work for a moment, creation would cease to exist.[7] Jesus is the sustainer of all things in heaven and earth, visible and invisible, holding all things together even when they seem to be falling apart.

Two months after he was confronted by Emma, Steve was wracked by guilt and shame, and he finally confessed his adulterous affair. Though she'd suspected and known what was coming for a while, Emma felt nauseated, almost passing out as she heard Steve utter, in what seemed like slow motion, the dreaded words, "I cheated on you." As if his confession weren't hurtful enough, Emma was blindsided by what he said next. Steve told her that he wasn't sure he wanted to be married to her anymore. He continued, "Bella makes me feel something I haven't felt for some time in our marriage."

Emma barely remembers what happened next. Her vision blurred and Steve's voice became muffled. After her initial shock began to subside and Emma regained her senses, she found Steve pacing back and forth in the garage. She told him to pack his bags and go. She needed some space to breathe and think. Steve grabbed a suitcase, packed, and was out the door within thirty minutes. As Emma watched his car head down the street, she fell to the floor sobbing. Her life flashed before her eyes, and her thoughts raced ahead to what seemed like the inevitable. *All of our dreams are shattered. Our marriage will end, and there's no hope of ever having kids with Steve.*

At once, their house, where she'd imagined raising kids and growing old together, became a dreadful reminder of her husband's betrayal. *No more birthdays and anniversaries to celebrate together. No more meaningful talks over coffee. No more opportunities to dream.*

What would she tell her parents? What would she say to their pastors and friends at church? Shame sunk its claws into Emma with each thought and unanswered question. Sorrow enveloped her more and more with each loss she envisioned.

If Jesus holds everything together, why does our world sometimes fall apart? Is he only holding the planets and atoms together, but not our lives? Where is Jesus when dreams shatter, marriages fail, and diseased or aging bodies break down? Such questions can only be answered by looking at God's story and not merely at our circumstances.

The Bible tells us that God knew about shattered dreams, broken marriages, disease, and death long before he breathed life into each of us (Psalm 139:16). You may ask, "If he knew about these things ahead of time, why did he allow them to happen?" It's a good question. But God doesn't give us an immediate answer. Rather, he calls us to trust his wisdom: "He made the earth by his power; he founded the world by his wisdom and stretched out the heavens by his understanding" (Jeremiah 51:15). When the dilemmas and mysteries arise, we live in the tension of reality. We must fully acknowledge the hard and painful realities of life, *and* we must also fully declare God's goodness and love. God doesn't want us to minimize or deny our pain, but he also doesn't want us to minimize or deny his great love. These two realities can be true at the same time.

As we look at the realities of the fall in chapters 6 and 7, we'll discover that these examples are just some of the ways that evil impacts God's good creation. The evil that is in us, around us, and that has been done to us accounts for the pain and heartache we've experienced, but evil's power doesn't negate Jesus's ability to hold all things together. It may seem that everywhere we look evil is doing damage, but the fall is only one part of God's story. God knows the extent of evil we experience, and he also knows his plans.

The good news is that the fall is not the end of God's story. Knowing the ways evil would impact you throughout your life, God sent his Son from heaven to earth for you. God is not the author of evil, but he uses the evil in this world to accomplish his good purposes (Genesis 50:20).

You may ask, "Why does God use evil for good? Why can't he only use good for good?" This is another mystery where we need to trust God's wisdom. When we look at the story of redemption (chapters 8–11), we'll see that God doesn't explain why he allowed evil to enter the world, but he does offer a cure.[8] God doesn't answer all of our questions, but he offers all of Christ, the Creator of the universe, who knows you and all of your days. In the tension of the evil and good you experience, Jesus reminds you that he is able to sustain not only the universe but your personal world as well. Jesus holds you close to his heart (Isaiah 40:11).

You may say, "It feels like my world is falling apart." But Jesus is your Good Shepherd, and he personally knows the pain of rejection, the anguish of betrayal, the agony of abuse, and the sting of death. He tells us that we will have trouble in this world, but that he has overcome the world (John 16:33). He can hold you together. Jesus doesn't promise to take away our dark valleys; instead, he promises to be with us and comfort us through the darkness. Even though you may feel like everything is caving in on you, he promises that no amount of evil can ever separate you from his love (Romans 8:38–39). Jesus holds you together with his love.

When we take a glimpse at consummation (chapter 12), we'll see that Christ will one day destroy evil's very existence. No longer will there be a dual reality of good and evil as we know it now, but Christ's love will reign over all. This gives us hope in our present struggles. As Paul says, "For our light and momentary troubles are achieving for us an eternal glory that far outweighs them all. So we fix our eyes not on what is seen, but on what is unseen, since what is seen is temporary, but what is unseen is eternal" (2 Corinthians 4:17–18). God calls you to trust him and to keep your eyes on Jesus through both the good and bad times. As you do, Jesus will hold you and your story together as he reframes how you see and understand your life and your relationships, as he restores your soul, and as he redeems your story. As he does so, he will conform you more and more into Christ's image with each step of faith.

For All These Reasons, Jesus Is Your Hope

Given your story or your present circumstances, you may struggle to wrap your mind around the powerful reality that Jesus rules and reigns over all creation. The enemy may be seeking to convince you that your anxiety or sorrow will never go away, that your circumstances will never change, or that your story will always define you. His goal is for you to lose hope. But if all things were made in, through, and for Jesus—if he holds all things together—then it's possible for all things to be restored and re-created through him as well.

Emma had begun to lose hope. Grief and shame left numerous doubts in her heart about God's goodness and his ability to change her husband and save her marriage. As her doubts intensified over the weeks, she found herself confused, not even knowing what to pray. At times, she drifted into apathy, losing her desire to pray or to open her Bible.

Emma pulled away from family and friends who had sought to comfort and love her. When her best friend, Alice, was finally able to get her out of the house to grab coffee, she asked Emma, "What do you need right now?" Emma burst into tears, "I just want the pain to go away. I want to get my life back to how it was before all of this happened!" Emma continued to spiral down. She questioned why Steve didn't think she was enough. She wondered if her desire to have a baby pushed him aside. And she questioned whether there was any hope for them, for her.

Alice's mind raced as she listened to her best friend share deeply and honestly. She felt hopeless in caring for Emma. Alice didn't have any definitive answers for her. She couldn't change Emma's circumstances, and she certainly couldn't fix Steve. As she listened, a question kept circling in her head, "What *does* Emma need right now? What or who can make a difference in what seems like an impossible situation?"

Shift Your Gaze to Your Creator

Think back through the realities of the creation story outlined in this chapter and the last. What truths would help both Emma and Alice navigate through this storm? What difference does it make to know that God created us for communion with him? Is it possible for Emma to know, experience, and image him in the aftermath of Steve's adultery and the throes of her heartache? What difference can Jesus make when Emma's world seems to be falling apart?

The same answers you would give to Emma are true for us all, whatever the particulars of our stories and struggles. Jesus knows all of your pain and brokenness, and he invites you to draw near. Jesus says, "Come to me, all of you who are weary and carry heavy burdens, and I will give you rest. Take my yoke upon you. Let me teach you, because I am humble and gentle at heart, and you will find rest for your souls. For my yoke is easy to bear, and the burden I give you is light" (Matthew 11:28–30 NLT).

Jesus, your Creator, invites you to place your hope in him because he is your life. Since all things were made through and for Jesus, it's possible for everything to be restored through him as well. Look at him instead of at your circumstances. Listen to his wisdom instead of worldly speculations. Trust his understanding instead of your own. Be confident in his purposes. He is your Good Shepherd; he cares for you.

God's Invitation

Spend some time in God's Word. Open your heart to God and share with him how you may be struggling with who you are or your purpose. Or share what aspects of your life seem to be falling apart.

Read Psalm 146 slowly once or twice as you keep in mind what you shared with God. How does this passage give you hope and help in your struggles? What truths reassure you that Jesus can hold all things, including you and your world, together?

CHAPTER 6
THE FALL: EVIL KEEPS US FROM LOVE

NIKKI FELT better than ever. Her renewed relationship with Christ has infused her soul with life. She's found herself more joyful and thankful, and her friends have noticed the change in her attitude.

Then, one weekend, Nikki hung out with Kris, her friend who had invited Nikki to church several months before. The two women planned to catch up over pizza at Kris's house and then watch a movie. God had been doing so much in each of their lives. As they shared a meal, they also shared how grateful they were for how they were experiencing God through his Word and their small group at church.

"Work is still hectic," Nikki said. "But I'm thankful that it no longer drives my life."

When the last bite of pizza was gone and they felt caught up on one another's lives, they eagerly shifted to movie mode. Kris made some popcorn; then they relaxed on the sofa, sharing a blanket.

Half an hour into the movie, Nikki felt short of breath; she experienced what felt like a panic attack. The movie they were watching included a scene in which a guy sexually assaulted the main female character at a party. As Nikki watched what was happening on the screen, she was taken back to something that happened to her as a teenager in London. She began to relive what she had seen and heard during her own assault.

Kris could see just how shaken Nikki was, and she figured something in the movie had triggered her, but she didn't know what. Nikki started crying, and Kris brought her some tissues.

"What happened?" asked Kris. Nikki didn't respond.

Kris waited for what seemed like hours before she tentatively asked Nikki if something she had seen in the movie sparked her reaction. Nikki's fright and anxiety were obvious. Nikki took a deep breath and started to say something, but then she buried her face in a pillow and wept some more.

"You don't have to say anything," Kris reassured her friend. "But if you want to talk, I'll listen. And I'll be by your side regardless of what you share."

After about an hour, Nikki took another deep breath. With her tissue in hand, she slowly recounted for Kris events that she had never shared with anyone before. Nikki shared how when she was seventeen, she and some friends had snuck into a party at the nearby university. Nikki got into a conversation with a guy who had caught her eye. After a few minutes, he asked her if she was hungry. They left the party to grab some fish-and-chips. But instead of driving to the restaurant, this guy pulled off the road into the woods and forced himself on her.

Nikki continued shakily, "I screamed and pushed him away, but . . . but . . . he was stronger than me and no one was around to hear me scream. After he finished, I punched him in the face and escaped from the car."

Nikki told Kris how she'd run up to the road and waved for help. Her friends, who were driving to look for her, saw her and pulled over. They asked her what happened. Nikki had told them that some dodgy guy from the party tried to force himself on her, but that she had gotten away before anything happened.

"I was too ashamed to say what had really happened," said Nikki. "I was afraid my parents would find out if I said anything to my friends."

All of Creation Is Broken by Evil

Abuse, loneliness, anxiety, and betrayal were not part of the life that God wanted for his people. Ever since Adam and Eve's sin, every person has been overcome by sin's destructive nature. The result is that we are broken, and we live in a broken world. We experience the brokenness of evil against us and within us. Our souls are broken by the evils of self-love and vanity. Our relationships are broken through lying, conflict, jealousy, rage, selfish ambition, division, neglect, envy, disrespect, manipulation, isolation, assault, and murder. Our souls are further impacted when we respond to evil with the common struggles—fantasy, shame, guilt, fear, anger, and sorrow. Our communion with God is broken by sin. As a result, doubts, disobedience, and relentless spiritual warfare keep us from knowing, experiencing, and imaging God. Our bodies are broken by disease, dysfunction, and death. Even creation groans as it experiences the brokenness of natural disasters, droughts, pollution, and infestations (Romans 8:19–23).

We know that this brokenness can cause us to doubt God's love, and that our doubts impact how we love others. We know that our brokenness must be addressed. But before we begin to unpack God's solution for our brokenness, we need to explore the story of how evil and brokenness entered the world.

A Clash of Kingdoms

Our brokenness began before the creation of heaven and earth with a clash of kingdoms. This clash began with a battle for glory. Satan clashed with God in the heavens; in his pride, he wanted to be worshiped like God, but he lost that battle and was cast out from heaven (Isaiah 14:12–14). We see this battle for worship and glory continue when Jesus faced off with Satan in the wilderness. The devil tempted Jesus to worship him by offering a kingdom that wasn't his to give, a promise on which he could not ultimately deliver: "The devil led [Jesus] up to a high place and showed him in an instant all the kingdoms of the world. And he said to him, 'I will give you all their authority and splendor; it has been given to me, and I can give it to anyone I want to. If you worship me, it will all be yours'" (Luke 4:5–7).

God wants his creation—from angels to humanity—to worship only him. He wants his people to give him glory with their entire being. But just as he did with Jesus, Satan seeks, with half-truths and empty promises, to lure our affections elsewhere. He would have us trade God's glory for lesser glories.

The clash of kingdoms was also a battle for love. Satan's mission has always been to undermine God, and one of Satan's primary strategies is to undermine and distort how people know and experience God's love. Satan's strategy makes sense, because God intends that his love compel and control us, so we will live for him and not for ourselves. If Satan can undermine God's love in our hearts and affections, he will succeed in undermining the very thing God designed to give our lives direction, meaning, and motivation.

As we've already seen, the clash between the kingdoms of good and evil—the battle for glory and love—spilled over from God and Satan into God's creation. When God created the first man and woman, God gave them a lush garden to live in and worthy words to live by. "The LORD God commanded the man, 'You are free to eat from any tree in the garden; but you must not eat from the tree of the knowledge of good and evil, for when you eat from it you will certainly die'" (Genesis 2:16–17). Essentially, God told the man and woman, "Enjoy life as I created it. Enjoy my garden and everything in it. Enjoy one another. Enjoy your calling to fill the earth and govern it. And most importantly, enjoy life with me, because I created you to live and flourish in my presence."

But then evil crept into the garden: "Now the serpent was more crafty than any of the wild animals the LORD God had made. He said to the woman, 'Did God really say, "You must not eat from any tree in the garden?"'" (Genesis 3:1). Instead of trusting God, Adam and Eve listened to Satan and ate from the tree of the knowledge of good and evil. Even though they *knew God*, Adam and Eve chose to *know evil.* Once they knew evil, they *did evil* as well. Adam and Eve did not physically die immediately after eating the fruit. The real death promised was separation from God.

Because they were the stewards of creation, Adam and Eve's decision sent shock waves throughout the earth, causing the entire world to experience death and separation from God's design. Like acid rain ruins all it touches, sin set in motion a curse that damaged everything and everyone. Now our lives are filled with sin and suffering.

Often, it's hard to distinguish between sin and suffering. In your *suffering*, you can sinfully respond to the darkness and heartache. In your *sinning*, you are suffering since you are not living as God created you to live. Consequently, your *struggles* involve both suffering and sin. Ultimately, such struggles confuse us about God's love. In our pain and darkness, we doubt God and fail to experience his love.

The Clash Within

Let's take a closer look at the dynamics of sin and suffering in our own hearts—at how the ancient clash of kingdoms is waged in our everyday lives.

The Enemy's mission is to blind people to God's reality, to blind people from knowing and experiencing God's glory and love: "The god of this age has blinded the minds of unbelievers, so that they cannot see the light of the gospel that displays the glory of Christ, who is the image of God" (2 Corinthians 4:4).

This is why you should never judge anyone who refuses to believe. Your family and friends who are unbelievers are not merely apathetic or uninterested in God, but they are powerless to believe on their own. Satan blinds hearts and minds so they *cannot* see their Creator. Apart from God's Spirit, we are, as John Owen wrote, "incapable of believing. Music cannot please a deaf man, nor can beautiful colors impress a blind man."[9] Only when God draws us near with his kindness, awakens us with his love, and opens our eyes with his truth, will his Spirit bring us from death to life.

But even those who profess to know and follow Jesus can battle to believe God and his Word. The writer of Hebrews warns, "See to it, brothers and sisters, that none of you has a sinful, unbelieving heart that turns away from the living God" (Hebrews 3:12). Whether you realize it or not, we all struggle with a sinful, unbelieving heart that is fully capable of turning away from God. Your outward struggles often make you aware of your inward struggles. Jesus told us, "It is what comes from inside that defiles you. For from within, out of a person's heart, come evil thoughts, sexual immorality, theft, murder, adultery, greed, wickedness, deceit, lustful desires, envy, slander, pride, and foolishness. All these vile things come from within; they are what defile you" (Mark 7:20–23 NLT).

We also suffer when we are confronted with the brokenness of the world. When we witness evil, something happens deep within us. There can be a visceral response that courses through us, along with disgust, sadness, fear, anger, and even overwhelming hopelessness. When we experience evil firsthand, e.g., hurtful remarks from a friend, or racial injustice, or malicious abuse, our heart and soul are furthered damaged in immeasurable and lasting ways.

Mark became a Christian at an early age but didn't realize the battle within him until he was older. As early as he could remember, his adoptive parents would take the family to church on Sundays—then back again on Wednesday nights. At home, his parents would read the kids stories from a children's Bible. He loved the stories of David and Goliath, Jonah and the big fish, and Daniel in the lion's den. He learned the stories of God's people battling against evil. Mark's parents also wanted to help the kids have strength for spiritual battle—so they would memorize Bible verses weekly; writing them on index cards and taping them around the house where everyone could see them as they went about their day.

When Mark was twelve years old, he stumbled upon his big brother's pornographic magazine. It was hidden in the corner of the closet where Mark had been looking for his brother's baseball glove. Mark opened the magazine with excitement and fear. He saw things he had never seen before, and he'd never experienced his body responding the way it did as he gazed at the images. Little did he know but this accidental exposure would lead to years of intentional scheming and acting out.

During his high school years, Mark spent hours on his computer. Mark's parents had software that blocked explicitly pornographic sites and tracked and reported any suspicious browsing, but he still looked at websites where he would find images of women who were dressed provocatively. He also memorized movies that had sexual scenes or brief nudity, and he would secretly watch those film clips again and again. Knowing such pleasures were sinful, Mark struggled to stop, but the conviction he experienced was outweighed by his fleshly desires.

During college, where Mark had more freedom, he started hanging out in chat rooms, satisfying his lust through real-time interactions. Mark found himself obsessed with porn, and he noticed over the years that this struggle made him uncomfortable around women. His mind would quickly make them objects of his lust. He wanted to find a wife because he believed the lie that when he did get married, his struggles with porn would go away. Mark's chronic struggle left him exhausted, defeated, and confused. Because he was unable to stop this particular sin struggle despite countless confessions, accountability groups, desperate prayers, and Scripture memorization, he began to doubt his salvation. His sense of shame and guilt was overwhelming.

Our Heart Struggles

We all struggle in similar ways with the impact of evil brought about by the fall.

First, in response to the evil in and around us, we all face to some degree the *common struggles*—the fantasy, guilt, shame, fear, anger, and sorrow (see chapter 1)—that Adam and Eve first faced after the fall.

Second, we experience *relational struggles* with others. We can experience a wide range of relational brokenness—fighting, loneliness, disrespect, disregard, family dysfunction, physical and sexual abuse, or even the death of loved ones. As a result, we might respond with distrust, self-protection, defensiveness, suspicion, isolation, or avoidance. We will explore how the fall further impacts our relationships in chapter 7.

Third, we all wrestle with *faith struggles* as we strive to live with God in this broken world. These are the faith struggles you might experience:

- *Battles with doubt.* You can doubt God's presence, promises, and power. You might say: *God, where are you? God, do you care for me? Do you love me? I believe God's promises for others, but not for me. God, you can't change me . . . or my spouse. God, I doubt you can protect me or provide for me.*

- *Battles with despair.* When life changes for the worse, and you can't see any light at the end of the tunnel, you can battle despair. You can lose hope when your circumstances or relationships don't improve. You might think: *Why hasn't God changed me or my circumstances? Things will never change. Why won't God give me what I ask for?*

- *Battles with distance.* You can also think or feel that God is far from you. You can struggle in your faith when it seems God hasn't heard or answered your prayers. You might feel the distance when you are hopeless, thinking that he has given up on you. You may even turn your back on God and harden your heart toward him. In these situations, you might say: *How can I love a God who allowed that to happen? How can God love me after what I did? How can God love me after what was done to me? God doesn't hear or answer my prayers. God seems so far away.*

HEART STRUGGLES

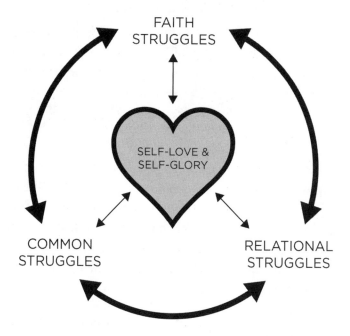

The diagram shows the reciprocal nature of our struggles. Common struggles can lead to relational struggles, and relational struggles can stir up common struggles in our hearts. Each of these can also result in faith struggles. And our faith struggles can give way to common struggles or relational struggles. All of these struggles are fueled by our bent toward self-love and self-glory. Because God created us to relate and respond to our circumstances, these struggles are not merely passive responses, but are active ways of relating and responding to life and to those around us.

Mark's Heart Struggles

Mark's loneliness and his feelings of not belonging stir up *shame* within him. He feels unloved, and he *fears* being alone for the rest of his life. His struggle with being given up for adoption prompts him to turn to *fantasy*. Mark daydreams about a version of his life where his parents never gave him up. He experiences deep *sorrow* for not being wanted by them. Mark also feels *guilt* over his struggle with pornography. He's *angry* that his efforts to change his behavior have been fruitless.

Over the years, Mark struggled to make friends as he always felt different from everyone. Even as an adult, he struggles with anxiety whenever he walks into a room full of people. Whenever someone doesn't acknowledge him as they pass in the hallways at work, Mark immediately wonders what he might have done wrong to offend them. As a result of these relational struggles, he has been experiencing faith struggles, doubting God's love for him. When he dwells on why his biological parents didn't want him, he finds himself sinking into despair. When his doubts and despair overwhelm him, God seems far away. At times, Mark wonders whether God has turned his back on him.

The Ongoing Reality of Spiritual Warfare

Further complicating the struggles of life is that, in this broken world, an evil trinity—the flesh, the world, and the devil—wage war daily against God and his people. We call this spiritual warfare.

Even as Christians, our sinful *flesh* battles against God's Spirit, prompting us to love ourselves more than we love God and others. The *world*, a culture that lives as if there is no God, feeds our insatiable desire to be the center of our kingdom.[10] Moreover, our Enemy knows our sinful condition and how susceptible we are to temptation. Nothing brings the *devil* greater joy than fueling doubt, confusion, and disobedience in God's people.

We need to remember that our struggles are not ultimately "against flesh and blood, but against the rulers, against the authorities, against the powers of this dark world and against the spiritual forces of evil in the heavenly realms" (Ephesians 6:12). The Enemy knows he can't separate us from the love of God, so he seeks to undermine anything and everything that keeps us from loving God and others. Satan employs four major schemes in this battle, but God counters each one.

1. The Enemy *deceives* us with lies about God, about others, and about ourselves. He seeks to keep us from believing God's truths and the realities revealed or promised in his Word (John 8:44; Revelation 12:9). To counter this, God's Spirit gives us wisdom and revelation so that we might know the truth about God and his Word better (Ephesians 1:17; Psalm 119).

2. The Enemy *distracts* us, seeking to use our confusion about God's Word, our suffering, the worries of life, or the deceit of wealth to lead us astray (Matthew 13:18–22). If we are thinking more about our circumstances than about the God who dwells within us or the spiritual warfare that surrounds us, the Enemy has accomplished his purpose. God speaks to our distraction when he commands us to remember, look up, gaze upon his beauty, and meditate upon his Word (Philippians 4:8; Colossians 3:1–2).

3. The Enemy *discourages* us, tempting us to believe that nothing will change or that the bad outweighs the good in life (Ezra 4:4; Nehemiah 6; Psalm 73:1–14). God counters this by speaking to our despair and calling us to not grow weary nor lose heart (Joshua 1:9; 2 Corinthians 4:1; Galatians 6:9; Hebrews 12:3).

4. Finally, the Enemy's deception, distraction, and discouragement can lead to *division* between God and us, or between others and us (Genesis 3:23; Ephesians 2:12 and Genesis 37:18–19; Galatians 5:15; Philippians 4:2). It's no surprise that God repeatedly commands us to pursue peace, be reconciled, and fight for unity and oneness (Psalm 34:14; Matthew 5:24; Romans 14:19; 2 Corinthians 5:19–20; Ephesians 4:3–6).

Our Faith Struggles Are Common, but Serious

As your faith struggles—doubts, despair, and distance—harden your heart toward God and keep you from experiencing his love, you might also become angry with him. Taking time to process what makes you angry is an essential part of spiritual warfare, knowing that while you are in darkness and pain, the enemy seeks to deceive you about God and divide you from him.

Remember, anger is a strong feeling of displeasure or hostility in response to someone or something that opposes what you value.[11] This understanding of anger should cause you to pause and consider why you are angry with God. When we get mad at God, we can take one of two extreme stances:

First, we might accuse God of not being good. We can blame him for the evil in the world and the bad things that happen, such as the death of a spouse or child, or a prolonged season of misfortune or misery, sickness, or loneliness.

Second, we might accuse God of not being loving. We accuse him of not caring because we know he could have prevented the evil we experienced; or because he did not choose to give us what we wanted.

We have to take our faith struggles seriously. If left unchecked, our doubts, despair, and distance will take a toll on how we live and love. We will lack joy when doubts erode our trust in God. We will lack peace when despair drains any sense of hope. We will struggle to know and experience God's love when we think God is distant or when we hold God at a distance. As a result, some of us may become cynical, discontented, even numb, as we settle for just surviving. Or, we can seek to control every aspect of our lives, convinced that no one else could take care of us better than ourselves.

Let's consider the psalmist's confident reflection: "We wait in hope for the LORD; he is our help and our shield. In him our hearts rejoice, for we trust in his holy name. May your unfailing love be with us, LORD, even as we put our hope in you" (Psalm 33:20–22).

When we trust that God is our help and shield, we can rejoice. When we wait in hope for the Lord to work according to his promises, we can pray without ceasing. When we rest in his unfailing love, we can give thanks in all circumstances.

The Battle Impacts Everyone, but the War Is Already Won

It's important to know that you are not the only one walking this war-torn road. No one is left unscathed in the battle with common struggles. Your heart struggles can keep you from loving others, holding you back from offering them the attention and care they deserve. The heart struggles of others impact you as well. If you have coworkers who struggle with unaddressed anger or sorrow, they may lash out and hurt you and others. If you have friends who struggle with fear and anxiety, they may become overly dependent upon you. Others may seek to cover up their insecurities by being arrogant, defensive, or competitive, making it difficult for others to love them. If you have a loved one who has been abused, the shame of their experience can bleed into your life, adding even more to your struggles.

Your struggles impact others, and theirs impact you. Knowing this reality shouldn't cause you guilt or lead you to assign blame. Instead, it should lead you to develop humility, compassion for others, and an awareness that this battle truly is bigger than you. God understands how people's lives intertwine and where your struggles impact one another. His story includes theirs too. That is why he commands you to encourage one another daily and to bear one another's burdens (Galatians 6:2).

Sin is devastating, but it is not the end of the story. The darkness of sin cannot eclipse God's glory. There is hope. Love came down from heaven to counteract evil's work. God's powerful love overcomes both sin's grip on you and the shame of sin committed against you. Sin still dwells within you, but the God of love also dwells within you through his Spirit. He is with you in every step of your journey. You may continue to fight battles, but the war is already won.

On your journey, it can be easy to spend most of your time and energy looking at the ugliness of sin, with only an occasional glance at the glory of God. You might focus on how you have sinned or how someone else has sinned against you, rather than focusing on how God loves you, has forgiven you, and is always with you through Jesus Christ.

But the good news is that you *can* face your struggles daily with the Holy Spirit's help, knowing that he has ultimately won the war against sin for you. He is the victor in this ancient clash of kingdoms. As you live in this fallen and broken world, God is calling out to you, "Come back to me, seek me, set your gaze on me, turn back to me and follow me." God is extending this sweet invitation to you every moment of every day. Even though you are prone to wander, prone to reject his glory and love, your God will continue to be your Shepherd.

God's Invitation

Spend some time with God through his Word. Open your heart to God and share with him how you may be struggling with sin in your heart, in your relationships, and with the sin in the world.

Read Isaiah 55 slowly once or twice as you consider your struggles. What does God promise as he invites you to draw near to him?

CHAPTER 7
THE FALL: SIN, TEMPTATION, AND BROKEN RELATIONSHIPS

STEVE EXPERIENCED a sense of freedom and relief when Emma kicked him out of the house. He no longer had to hide where he'd been or give her an account of his time. He moved in with Bella so he could fully enjoy his new love. They spent a lot of their time doing things Emma didn't enjoy—like taking spontaneous overnight trips and trying new dishes from different countries. Steve hadn't felt this happy in years, and he kept thinking about how he wished he had met Bella earlier. But even in this new paradise, everything wasn't at peace in Steve's heart. He would catch himself thinking about Emma as he fell asleep in different surroundings. His thoughts about her fluctuated between hurt and guilt. She made him feel like he was never good enough, but he knew how much he had hurt her. Emma had been his wife for nearly seven years.

Relationships Are Broken

Relationships can be the source of our greatest joy and deepest pain. Since the fall, the way people relate and respond to both God and one another has been distorted. We rebelled against God's authority, lied about it, and blamed one another. We cheat and steal. We're unfaithful to friends and to spouses and when we get caught, we do everything in our power to cover it up. In anger, people say stupid things over dinner or on the internet. In rage, people have even killed and gone to war with one another. The enmity and hostility that results between us and God as well as between us and one another across generations and nations is evil.

It's no wonder that relationships are hard. Period. The Enemy leverages our sins, creating hostility in our relationships and corrupting any sense of peace or unity. *It's not only that sin is found in every relationship, but also, sin is relational.*

Before God saved us, we were his enemies. We loved the darkness. As a result of Adam and Eve's rebellion against the Creator, we were born into sin. Even after being saved by grace, we still engage in evil through our sinful thoughts, self-focused emotions, wicked desires, and evil actions.

Since we can hide our sin from everyone else, we think we can also hide it from God. Others don't know our secret thoughts or the private desires in our hearts, but God does. Google and Facebook can track your keystrokes, and Alexa can record everything you say within earshot, but God knows what goes on in your heart and mind. He knows how you scheme to make yourself look better than your coworkers, or how you can manipulate a friend to get what you want. God hears the conversations you have with yourself and knows the sinful desires that get your heart racing as you gossip, and as you wrestle with bitterness, envy, and lust. God sees every click on your phone, every glance you take, every rude gesture, or judgmental eye roll. He knows how you spend every waking hour and the details of your dreams.

If we believe that God knows every detail of our life, why do we do what we shouldn't, and fail to do what we should (Romans 7:15)? There is a range of reasons that explains why we sin the way we do. In the best case, we may not realize that what we are doing is sinful. Or perhaps we give in to temptation after trying to resist it for some time. We can be swayed by friends or by social media to do what everyone else is doing. Or we can sin because we want what we want, but then feel bad after the temporary pleasure evaporates. In the worst case, we sin because we don't care what God thinks anymore.

But we need to remember two realities. First, sin is, and always will be, more powerful than you. Second, because of sin's power, only the Holy Spirit can enable us to live for God instead of for self.

How God Sees Our Sin

Regardless of why we sin today, God views sin the same way as he did in the Garden of Eden. Scripture uses three different Hebrew words for sin. The first is translated "transgression," and it describes defiance or rebellion. The second word is translated "iniquity," which means perversion, distortion, or twistedness. The last Hebrew word for sin is translated "missing the mark," and it describes how we fall short of God's commands and righteous standards. All of these ways to describe sin are helpful, and through all of these words, God wants us to understand that our sin means breaking our relationship with him.

King David committed sexual assault against and adultery with Bathsheba. Then, he proceeded to have her husband killed. Sometime later, the prophet Nathan confronted him with a parable that helped David see his grievous sin. Nathan asked David, "Why did you despise the word of the LORD by doing what is evil in his eyes?" (2 Samuel 12:9). This is how God sees sin: as despising his Word and doing evil.

Some of you may push back, thinking, "But I don't despise God's Word. I love the Bible." But our actions show otherwise. In Judges, God attributed Israel's cycle of sin to everyone doing what was right in their own eyes (Judges 21:25 ESV). Because of our sinful tendency toward self-trust, God commands us, "Trust in the LORD with all your heart and lean not on your own understanding; in all your ways submit to him, and he will make your paths straight. Do not be wise in your own eyes; fear the LORD and shun evil" (Proverbs 3:5–7). Take a moment and consider— what difference would it make if you began to see your pride, slander, unforgiveness, sinful anger, or lying as doing evil in God's eyes?

Evil offends God. When the Holy Spirit convicted David of his sins, David declared, "Against you, you only, have I sinned and done what is evil in your sight" (Psalm 51:4). When Israel demanded a king, God said to his prophet Samuel, "It is not you they have rejected, but they have rejected me as their king" (1 Samuel 8:7). In his first letter to the church in Thessalonica, Paul wrote, "Therefore, anyone who rejects this instruction does not reject a human being but God, the very God who gives you his Holy Spirit"

(1 Thessalonians 4:8). All sin offends God, because each sin involves a personal rejection of him. When we despise and reject God's Word, we despise and reject the One who spoke to us through the Word. Moreover, the Bible describes Jesus Christ *as* the Word (John 1:1; Revelation 19:13). So, every time we sin, we not only despise God's written Word, but we also despise Jesus Christ, the living Word.

Lastly, God sees our sin against him as adultery. "'But like a woman unfaithful to her husband, so you, Israel, have been unfaithful to me,' declares the LORD" (Jeremiah 3:20). "How I have been grieved by their adulterous hearts, which have turned away from me, and by their eyes, which have lusted after their idols" (Ezekiel 6:9). God sees our sin against him as adultery because he created us to love him first and foremost. He is our first love, and he requires our whole-hearted and pure devotion (Matthew 22:37; 2 Corinthians 11:3; Revelation 2:4).

Seeing our sin in these ways should disturb us. God knew in advance about our chronic unfaithfulness, and he wants us to know that we are more sinful than we could ever imagine.

But God wants us to know so much more. When we see the depths and darkness of our sin—when we become more aware of our arrogance and foolishness—we must also see that God doesn't intend this awareness to condemn us; rather, he wants us to grow in humility and become more dependent upon and desperate for him. Most importantly, God wants us to see the increasing heights of his love in contrast to the depths of our sinfulness. God knows about our sinfulness, but he fully covers it through Christ's finished work on the cross.

Christ established his everlasting covenant of love with us, and now his incomparable and selfless love compels us to respond to him with mutual love. Our love relationship with him enables us to delight in Jesus's Word and motivates us to obey him by faith.

Temptation and Sin

The fact that Christ has overcome sin doesn't make living in love and obedience easy. We still live under the curse of the fall. Doubt and discouragement can overshadow the incredible truths of the gospel, and, as a result, we can question God's love.

The Enemy knows God is the One who gives us life and the ability to live and love differently. Satan understands that he can't separate us from God's love. He knows he can't snatch us from the caring hands of our Heavenly Father, our Good Shepherd. But he does everything within his power to undermine our most important relationship.

Satan is at work in our lives to deceive us into giving in to temptation. Being tempted is not necessarily sin. Even Jesus was tempted by the devil. Temptation is any invitation to turn away from God, and it can be either external or internal in origin.

We see an example of *external temptation* in Joseph's story. Potiphar's wife tried to seduce Joseph on two separate occasions. Both times, he refused and fled from her sexual advances. Joseph refused her because he knew that giving in would not only betray his boss but would also be turning away from God. He told Potiphar's wife, "How then could I do such a wicked thing and sin against God?" (Genesis 39:9). External temptation leads to sin when a person gives in to that temptation and turns away from God by despising his Word and desiring or doing what is evil in God's eyes.

An *internal temptation* arises from the desires of our sinful flesh, and it should be confessed as sin. Internal temptations can be fleeting thoughts—like a momentary desire to lash out in rage or a lustful desire that arises from an unguarded glance. Internal temptations can also linger—a well-worn grudge, sexual desire for someone who is not your spouse, hopeless desires to end your own life, or obsessive thoughts about how to get your own way regardless of the means or consequences. David acted on his sexual desires and used his power to sleep with Bathsheba and kill her husband. Evil thoughts and inclinations in our hearts bear evil fruit, so we need to turn from and confess them.

Knowing that we will battle inward sinful desires and external temptations until Christ returns or we see him in glory, we need to cultivate contrary affections that are informed by God's love and his Word. Instead of acting out our story based on what we want, we need to rest in the strength that God offers us in *his* story. God created us to be compelled by his story of love.

Temptations Are Opportunities to Run to Jesus

The constant struggle to free yourself from unwanted thoughts and desires can be discouraging. You may even deceive yourself into thinking you have already sinned when you are tempted. So you label yourself hopeless and conclude that you should go ahead and act on the temptation.

Instead, God wants you to see temptation as a merciful reminder that you desperately need Jesus. Temptation can turn into a moment of victory through God's story. Let what the Enemy means for evil be used instead to turn your gaze toward Christ, who invites you to draw near to him for love that is better than life and peace this world can't give. See times of temptation as opportunities to grow in humility before God and dependence upon him.

Paul described it this way: "No temptation has overtaken you except what is common to mankind. And God is faithful; he will not let you be tempted beyond what you can bear. But when you are tempted, he will also provide a way out so that you can endure it" (1 Corinthians 10:13). God doesn't promise to take away temptation, nor does he promise that you will not sin in your temptation. What God promises in this passage is that he will help you to endure in faith through any temptation without falling away from him. You may endure certain temptations for a lifetime, but know that God has only allowed what will help you to grow in humble dependence upon Christ.

So, when you are tempted to sin, run to Jesus for refuge. Cry out to him. Run to Jesus through his Word and be reminded of his comforting presence and his life-giving promises. Instead of listening to the lies in your head or following the feelings in your heart, follow Christ through obedient faith so that you can abide in his love and experience his joy. He hasn't allowed more temptation to come your way than you can bear with his help. He stands ready to be your way of escape.

Sorrow and Sin

As we look back at the story of the fall, we see that Adam and Eve experienced sorrow immediately after sinning against God. They lost their sweet, intimate communion with God as he removed them from the garden, away from his presence. Ever since the fall, sin and sorrow have always gone hand in hand.

In his first letter to the Corinthians, Paul dealt with the church lovingly but directly. He spoke about how they condoned incest, relied on the courts to judge church matters, misused spiritual gifts that lead to disorder in worship, and profaned the Lord's Supper by allowing people to partake with gluttony and a lack of love.[12] As their father in the faith, Paul loved them enough to correct their practice, but he knew his words would bring them sorrow.

> Even if I caused you sorrow by my letter, I do not regret it. Though I did regret it—I see that my letter hurt you, but only for a little while—yet now I am happy, not because you were made sorry, but because your sorrow led you to repentance. For you became sorrowful as God intended and so were not harmed in any way by us. Godly sorrow brings repentance that leads to salvation and leaves no regret, but worldly sorrow brings death. (2 Corinthians 7:8–10)

Even unbelievers experience sorrow when they do something wrong. For both unbelievers and believers, sorrow stems from a conscience weighed down by a sense of guilt. We can also experience sorrow as we suffer the consequences of our actions—a loss of reputation, relationships, possessions, or even freedom through imprisonment. Worldly sorrow can drag us down to utter despair if we don't see any possibility of change. Worldly sorrow doesn't produce repentance, merely remorse for the wrongdoing, and, at best, a renewed commitment to do better. Tears and confession of sin alone don't equate to repentance.

But Paul tells us that godly sorrow leads to repentance. Such sorrow comes from God's work in us as his love pursues us and stirs our hearts, causing us to turn from evil, back to his loving arms. Godly sorrow is marked by Spirit-led brokenness that produces humility and a willingness to obey Christ, whatever the cost. In our rebellion, God invites us: "'Turn to me now, while there is time. Give me your hearts. Come with fasting, weeping, and mourning. Don't tear your clothing in your grief, but tear your hearts instead.' Return to the LORD your God, for he is merciful and compassionate, slow to get angry and filled with unfailing love. He is eager to relent and not punish" (Joel 2:12–13 NLT).

God's Love in Our Waywardness

One evening as he was lounging around the house with Bella, Steve felt an uneasiness permeate his soul. He dismissed the feeling at first. After all, he'd had a hard day at work, and they'd eaten lasagna for dinner. Over the next few days, however, Steve found himself thinking, "How did I get here? What am I doing?" As more time passed, Steve didn't feel like himself. He was fatigued, consumed with the difficulties of his life, and he struggled to remember details at work. He noticed a growing impatience with Bella. The differences between them that he used to find funny and cute now irritated him. One night after an argument about dishes in the sink, Bella turned to Steve and asked him if everything was okay. He said, confused, "I'm not sure what's going on." They kissed and headed up to bed.

The next morning, Steve got a text from Emma, who was paying all their bills, telling him to put more money in their bank account. Steve could feel anger rising deep inside. It took all he had to keep from screaming. Instead, he pursed his lips and let out a loud sigh of exasperation. He texted back: "I'm strapped for cash and can't afford to give you any more money." Then, Steve threw his phone across the room. Bella jumped out of bed when she heard the noise. She saw Steve slumped in a chair, crying—a sight she had never seen before. Concerned, she asked him what happened. Steve blurted out, "I can't do this anymore!" Then she asked, "What do you mean? I thought you loved me. I thought things were great between us." Exhausted and confused, Steve said that he couldn't keep up with his two different lives. "I'm thousands of dollars in debt, my body is falling apart, and my mind is so scattered that I am barely keeping my head above water at work."

Our hope for Steve is that God is bearing down on him—exposing Steve's adultery as well as his failure to love Christ and his wife. God loves us too much to allow us to live in ways that are contrary to how he designed us. God also bore down on David before he repented of his sins. David described the anguish he felt in his soul before he confessed his sins of assault, adultery, and murder: "When I refused to confess my sin, *my body wasted away, and I groaned all day long. Day and night your hand of discipline was heavy on me. My strength evaporated like water in the summer heat*" (Psalm 32:3–4 NLT, emphasis mine).

Take a moment to think about a remarkable truth: God's love for his people doesn't waver even in our ongoing adultery against him. Remember that he knows every day

of your life before you were born. He knows every temptation you would face, and every way you would choose evil
rather than choosing him. He hates sin, and it has no place
in his presence. Nevertheless, he chose to save you through
Christ and establish his unbreakable covenant of love with
you. Nothing you have done or will ever do surprises God.
Such gracious love doesn't permit you to continue sinning
against him because, as his child, your story has been united to Christ's story. You have been buried with and raised
to a new life in Christ so that you can be set free from sin
(Romans 6:1–7).

Instead of banishing us from his presence, as he did
with Adam and Eve in the Garden of Eden, God pursues
us when we stray like lost sheep. "For the LORD disciplines those he loves, and he punishes each one he ac-
cepts as his child" (Hebrews 12:6 NLT). He disciplines
us because his loving plans and desires for us never waiver
despite our ongoing struggle with sin. "God disciplines
us for our good, in order that we may share in his holiness" (Hebrews 12:10). Even though we often perceive it
differently, God's discipline shows us that the Maker of
heaven and earth is fighting for us. He wants us to have
a relationship with him. He wants us to share in his holiness and abide in his love.

Coming Out of the Dark

Steve had broken down crying in front of Bella. He knew he
needed help. On his way to work, he called his best friend,
Marcus, whom he had avoided ever since his affair had begun. Steve was desperate. He knew he couldn't stay with
Bella, but he didn't want to go home to Emma. He needed

a place to stay until he could clear his head. Fortunately, Marcus answered his phone, listened patiently, and asked Steve to meet him after work at their favorite brewery.

It didn't take long for Marcus to spot Steve sitting at a patio table outside the restaurant. Marcus was shocked at Steve's disheveled appearance; he seemed thinner than when they had last been together. When Steve offered to buy him a drink, Marcus saw that there were already two empty glasses on the table. For the next three hours, Marcus asked Steve questions and listened patiently to his answers. Some of Steve's responses seemed confused. He blamed Emma for their troubles, and he justified his affair by saying this was what he needed. Steve also stated that he had no desire to make things right with Emma. Given everything Steve shared, Marcus could see that Steve's sorrow was more about the consequences he was suffering, rather than turning to Christ in repentance. Steve paid the tab, and Marcus told Steve that he could stay at his place for two weeks. After that, he would need to find another place to live.

Our evil blinds and deceives us. King Solomon described the confusion that comes when we live in the dark, "But the way of the wicked is like deep darkness; they do not know what makes them stumble" (Proverbs 4:19). Steve's confusion stemmed from his decision to leave his wife and his deliberate choice to turn his back on Jesus, the Light of the World. In less extreme but equally damaging ways, we also walk in deep darkness when we live for ourselves rather than God, when we trust in our own understanding and not God's wisdom, when we doubt God and keep him at a distance, and when our hearts and minds stay centered on our circumstances instead of dwelling on God's realities by abiding in Christ.

But as God's people, we don't have to live in darkness. Just before Solomon described what it's like to live in the dark, he described the opposite way of living, "The path of the righteous is like the morning sun, shining ever brighter till the full light of day" (Proverbs 4:18). Take a moment to imagine starting a hike at sunrise. You see the sun peak over the horizon as you enjoy the dawn's cool air. You can enjoy the soft hues around the sun without hurting your eyes. Then, as you continue your trek, the sun rises higher in the sky, and you can feel the warmth of its rays. As the sun reaches its peak at noon, you break a sweat from its intense heat. At this point, you can only glance at the blazing sun before your eyes begin to burn. Our journey with Christ is similar. The longer we travel with him along paths of righteousness, the brighter our experience of him becomes (Psalm 23:3). We know and experience him more and more along our journey, and someday we'll see him face to face (1 Corinthians 13:12).

Steve had been in deep darkness for months during his affair, but he had begun to stray from Jesus long before that. It's no surprise that Steve is still confused after leaving Bella. Because he has been trying to live apart from Christ, evil has distorted the way he sees and understands life. Stories make no sense without God. But by God's grace, Marcus saw Steve's staying with him for a couple of weeks as an opportunity to journey alongside his friend and encourage him toward Jesus.

In the days that followed their meeting at the restaurant, Marcus noticed a progressive change in his friend.

They spent daily time together after work, reading and praying God's Word. Marcus watched his friend begin to resonate with God's truths. He had a front-row view of God's Spirit at work in Steve's heart. As Steve's thinking cleared, he began to see and own his sins against Emma and God. Steve was now on the path of repentance.

Reconciling Broken Relationships

The night before Steve left Marcus's place to move back into his parents' house, he decided that he wanted to talk with Emma and let her know that he wanted to fight for their marriage. He took a deep breath, and then he called her. She didn't pick up. He got a text from her, "Don't call me! I can't do this. You hurt me too much." At that moment, he realized that he could lose Emma. He also recognized that despite his repentance, his sin against his wife had real and lasting consequences.

When we look at God's story, we can see how sin damages relationships. Sin first broke our most important relationship, making it impossible to be right with God. Sin also breaks our human relationships when we fail to love one another. The good news is that God knows every way that evil impacts us and keeps us from love. God sent the Son from heaven into this world that is impacted by the fall in order to reconcile our broken relationship with God. He empowers us to reconcile our broken relationships with others through love and forgiveness.[13]

Though you continue to struggle with temptation and sin, God doesn't want you to live a defeated life, thinking you can't change. Don't be deceived by believing you have crossed the point of no return. No matter what you have done, or what has been done to you, God's promises remain. As you struggle to forgive those who have hurt you, don't despair, thinking you have to live in bitterness and hopelessness.

God's Invitation

Spend some time with God through his Word. Open your heart to God and share with him how you have rejected him and done evil in his eyes through your sin.

Read David's confession in Psalm 51 slowly once or twice as you consider your sins before God. How do David's confession and repentance differ from yours?

CHAPTER 8
REDEMPTION: JESUS RESTORES US WITH LOVE

SINCE THE evening she relived her sexual assault, Nikki has slipped into deep darkness. She is overwhelmed with the memories of what happened to her as a teenager. A flood of emotions accompanies the horrid details she can't seem to get out of her mind. As Nikki replays the attack in her mind, she finds herself asking why it happened to her and what she could have done to stop it. She struggles with guilt over putting herself in that situation. She still feels defiled, and she battles a sense of shame, wondering what her friends and family would think of her if they found out what really happened. Nikki notices that she is more impatient with her friends when they don't listen to her or when they seem to take advantage of her generosity. She lashes out in anger when other drivers speed or cut her off in traffic. She has installed a security system, fearing that someone could be in the house when she returns from work or might break in while she sleeps. She is filled with anxiety at bedtime because she's had nightmares about the assault and about other terrifying situations in which she is attacked or killed.

The Darkness in Your Story and God's Story

Evil can traumatize and enslave us with thoughts of endless fearful scenarios. We often respond by expressing a need for control and self-protection. We can be blinded with emotions that make lies feel like reality, causing us to dismiss the truth and spiral downward. Our feelings can also drive us to desire what is evil and wrong. When we believe the lies that sometimes fill our heads, despair from the pain and brokenness will fill our hearts. In our hopelessness, we can lose the desire for what is good and right.

Nikki's heart had begun to fill with despair and fear. Where can she look for help in the midst of this darkness? Where can she turn for hope when she feels overwhelmed and helpless? How will she ever heal from the debilitating influence of her past, painful experience?

Like Nikki, you may have past experiences that make your whole world feel dark. The darkness and depression may last for an extended season, or it may reoccur at the same time each year. You feel like you are drowning in darkness because the pain permeates deep in your soul. With this darkness comes a *fear* of the unknown and anxiety over endless unknown outcomes. You may be weighed down with *sorrow* over something you've lost, regret over something you should have done, or *guilt* over something you should never have done. *Shame* can drag you down into a pit of self-loathing where a sense of being unworthy and unloved leaves you in despair. You can become desperate for something—anything—that will change your circumstances, help you to feel differently, or take your mind off the pain (*fantasy*). Or, you might become complacent as you see your hopes and dreams fading away like a mirage.

The darkness seems suffocating. Your *doubts* drain your faith, *despair* eclipses hope, and a sense of *distance* from God and others leaves you feeling alone and defenseless.

God understands the power of evil, the deception of darkness, and our weakness in this fallen world. God begins the creation story with a desolate scene: "Now the earth was formless and empty, darkness was over the surface of the deep." Then, he closes this dismal description with striking intentionality by saying: "And the Spirit of God was hovering over the waters" (Genesis 1:2). Creation began when God entered the darkness.

At the end of God's story, we see a vastly different scene. In the new heavens and new earth, God's city "does not need the sun or the moon to shine on it, for the glory of God gives it light, and the Lamb is its lamp. . . . There will be no more night. They will not need the light of a lamp or the light of the sun, for the Lord God will give them light. And they will reign for ever and ever" (Revelation 21:23; 22:5). When we consider both of these accounts, it's comforting that God is present and active both in utter darkness and in the brilliance of his glory.

Jesus Came to Overcome the Darkness

Nikki's life had been turned upside down by her traumatic memories, and as a result, she battled nightly insomnia. One night, as she tossed and turned in bed, Nikki decided to get up, brew a cup of chamomile tea, and open her Bible. She pulled out her reading plan, which guided her to turn to John 8. As Nikki emerged from the haze of sleeplessness, a verse caught her eye: "Again Jesus spoke to them, saying, I am the light of the world. Whoever follows me will never walk in darkness, but will have the light of life" (John 8:12 ESV).

Nikki was taken back by the boldness of Jesus's declaration. She sat back in her chair, took a sip of tea, and reflected on Jesus's self-proclaimed identity as the "light of the world." As she read the rest of the verse, she felt a surge of peace as the light of Christ pierced the fortified darkness that had tormented her. Nikki experienced the presence of Christ, felt her body relax, and was able to take a deep breath. She felt a weight lift from her as she meditated on Jesus's promise that "whoever follows [him] will never walk in darkness, but will have the light of life." She envisioned a life where the darkness would no longer dominate her as she followed the Light of the World. As Nikki continued to dwell on the hope-filled realities of this passage, she began to feel drowsy. She took one final sip of tea, turned off the light, and went back to bed where she slept soundly until morning.

In the middle of his story, God did something unimaginable and extraordinary. He knew his people were helpless against the power of sin and blinded by the schemes of the Enemy. God knew his people could not save themselves. So, compelled by love, the Father sent his Son into the darkness, into the fallen world, to save us, to restore and give rest to fallen souls that had been damaged by sin. John describes Jesus's entrance into our world like this, "In him was life, and that life was the light of all mankind. The light shines in the darkness, and the darkness has not overcome it" (John 1:4–5). Since the first man and woman sinned against God, the darkness of evil has overcome humanity. But the darkness can never overcome the Light. The darkness was dispersed as Love himself entered into our story to rescue us.

Jesus Came to Destroy the Devil's Work

Jesus willingly obeyed his Father even though he knew the great humiliation, trauma, and death he would suffer in order to rescue God's people. John writes, "In the beginning was the Word, and the Word was with God, and the Word was God. He was with God in the beginning. Through him all things were made; without him nothing was made that has been made" (John 1:1–3). John references the creation story to help us see the extraordinary measures God took to redeem us. God sent his Son into the world the Son himself had made. But "though the world was made through him, the world did not recognize him. He came to that which was his own, but his own did not receive him" (John 1:10–11). Why did people respond to Jesus in this way? John explains, "Light has come into the world, but people loved darkness instead of light because their deeds were evil" (John 3:19). We were not created to know evil, thus, the sin in and around us will always overpower and overwhelm us if we try to live apart from Christ. The darkness of sin reorients our understanding, hijacks our emotions, and defiles our desires so that we live contrary to God's will. Instead of knowing and loving God with all our heart, soul, mind, and strength, we love the darkness and hate the light "for fear that [our evil] deeds will be exposed" (John 3:20).

The good news is that God is well aware of the devil's power. He knows how evil impacts us. God is not only aware of the Enemy's schemes, but he took decisive action: "The reason the Son of God appeared was to destroy the devil's work" (1 John 3:8). What is the devil's work? The devil seeks to undermine how we see God and experience his love. He seeks to undermine our faith and trust in God's goodness. If the devil can distort how we see God, cause us to doubt God's Word, and make us numb or apathetic to his love, then we will live for ourselves instead of living for God. The devil can't harm God himself, so he works to deceive and destroy us. He seeks to influence the way we live and love so that we relate to God and others with sinful attitudes and actions. Ultimately, the devil works to undermine our communion with God so that we will fail to love God and others. His work includes the damage and trauma done to our souls by the evil desires within us, the sin we have committed, and the evil committed against us. God is fully aware of all these ways that sin disorders our souls, and this is why he sent the Son. As we look to Christ, we see that our communion with God can never be broken, his Word never fails, his love is boundless, and one day all the devil's power will be taken away.

Jesus Came to Restore Our Souls

Along with his work of defeating the devil, Jesus came to restore our souls. God's saving intentions include a desire to comfort us in our troubles and bring restoration to our souls. Many passages speak about God's intentional comfort (Isaiah 40:11; 2 Corinthians 1:3–4; 7:6–7) and how our Good Shepherd restores our souls (Psalm 23:3; Hosea 6:2; 1 Peter 5:10). In Isaiah, God declares his promise to comfort and restore us with these words:

> The Spirit of the Sovereign LORD is on me, because the LORD has anointed me to proclaim good news to the poor. He has sent me to bind up the brokenhearted, to proclaim freedom for the captives and release

from darkness for the prisoners, to proclaim the year of the LORD's favor and the day of vengeance of our God, to comfort all who mourn, and provide for those who grieve in Zion—to bestow on them a crown of beauty instead of ashes, the oil of joy instead of mourning, and a garment of praise instead of a spirit of despair. They will be called oaks of righteousness, a planting of the LORD for the display of his splendor. (Isaiah 61:1–3)

Jesus's mission was not only to provide the means for our salvation, but he came from heaven to earth to be the means for our sanctification. In other words, Jesus came not only to reconcile our broken relationship with God, but he also came to restore our traumatized souls. Only Jesus Christ can bind hearts that have been broken by betrayal and abandonment. Only Jesus can free us from the thoughts and spiraling emotions that come with shame and fear. Only Jesus can release us from the darkness of despair and satisfy our thirst for revenge with his promise of vengeance and justice. Only Jesus can comfort us in our grief and crown us with his beauty and joy. In our instability and uncertainty, only Jesus can anchor us with the deep roots of his love.

After being tested in the wilderness, Jesus went to Nazareth, entered the synagogue, and read the passage from Isaiah 61:1–3. He rolled up the scroll, sat down, and declared, "Today this scripture is fulfilled in your hearing" (Luke 4:21). Jesus was confident in his ability to save us from the sins that broke our relationship with God and to restore us from the evil that damages our soul. He knew why he was sent from heaven to earth, and he knew what he had to do to accomplish his mission.

Jesus Came to Suffer for Us

During his commute home on the train each day, Mark had been reading John's first letter. When he got to 1 John 4, he read, "This is how God showed his love among us: He sent his one and only Son into the world that we might live through him. This is love: not that we loved God, but that he loved us and sent his Son as an atoning sacrifice for our sins" (1 John 4:9–10). At that moment, all of Mark's doubts about God's love for him vanished.

Mark saw how Christ's suffering led to his forgiveness. He experienced the bittersweet nature of true forgiveness. Seeing Christ's sacrifice, he knew the depth of his sin in a greater way but also knew God's overwhelming love in spite of his sin—even his struggle with pornography. He was able to taste the goodness of the Lord. God's love became more real to him. Mark sat back, his body relaxed, and he took a deep breath. The stresses of the day seemed to wash away. He was beginning to understand the words of the psalmist who proclaimed, "your unfailing love [is] my comfort" (Psalm 119:76).

Like Mark, we were created to know and experience God's love. More times than not, we are overwhelmed by life while being underwhelmed by God. Even though we can describe stress's impact on our body and soul, God's people can overlook how God's love, joy, and peace can be experienced. Believe it or not, abiding in the love of Christ is meant to counteract evil's impact on our souls and bodies.

When Jesus came, he knew that his mission to save and serve God's people would include suffering. He would be despised and rejected by the very people he created. After his arrest, he was abused both verbally and physically so that he was "disfigured beyond that of any human being" (Isaiah 52:14). Then, on the cross, Jesus encountered his greatest trial. Others have suffered physically in ways that were similar to the bodily torture Jesus experienced. In fact, two thieves were crucified next to him. But Jesus experienced ultimate suffering in three ways:

First, Jesus took upon himself the sins of the whole world (1 John 2:2). Consider the burden you feel when you've done something wrong. The sense of guilt and disgust can be more than you can handle. Consider what it feels like to bear the weight of an opponent taunting and tormenting you. The sense of shame can be overwhelming. Now, multiply what you experience personally by the number of people in the world throughout human history. Imagine what Jesus must have experienced. Paul says, "God made him who had no sin to be sin for us, so that in him we might become the righteousness of God" (2 Corinthians 5:21).

Second, Jesus absorbed God's wrath. Hurricane-force winds blow so hard that they pummel buildings and tear them apart. If a twenty-foot wave crashed down on you, its driving force would push the air out of your lungs and send you tumbling down to the ocean's floor. But these natural occurrences capture only a fraction of what Jesus experienced when he absorbed the fury of God's wrath for our transgressions. He endured the full measure of God's righteous anger against our sin until God's holiness and justice was fully satisfied. Jesus suffered God's wrath so that he could reconcile and restore us. Isaiah prophesied these words about Jesus: "He was pierced for our transgressions, he was crushed for our iniquities; the punishment that brought us peace was on him, and by his wounds we are healed" (Isaiah 53:5).

Finally, Jesus was forsaken by the Father. Darkness covered the land, starting at noon, as Jesus bore the crushing weight of the world's sin and suffered the unbearable torment of God's wrath. After three hours, he cried out in agony and anguish, "My God, my God, why have you forsaken me?" (Matthew 27:46). This cry was not a declaration of doubt about the Father's love, nor was it a cry of confusion about what he was experiencing. But for a moment never to be repeated, the Father turned his face away from his Son—not out of displeasure (because Jesus perfectly obeyed his Father's will) but because God's "eyes are too pure to look on evil" (Habakkuk 1:13). At that moment, Jesus did not consciously experience the deep, intimate fellowship he'd always known and enjoyed.

Let's not miss the beauty amid the darkness of Jesus's extreme suffering. Two realities were true at this moment: First, as Charles Spurgeon put it, "Jesus Christ was forsaken of God because we deserved to be forsaken of God."[14] Jesus willfully suffered temporary separation from God so that we would not suffer eternal separation. Because of Jesus's selfless sacrifice, we can declare with confidence that nothing "will be able to separate us from the love of God that is in Christ Jesus our Lord" (Romans 8:39). Second, before he took his final breath, Jesus cried out, "Father, into your hands I commit my spirit" (Luke 23:46). This cry revealed his unwavering trust in the guardian of his soul and his confidence that he would once again experience sweet, intimate communion with God. As John Piper reflects, Jesus "had embedded in his soul both the horrors of the moment of abandonment, and he had embedded in his soul 'for the joy that was set before him.'"[15] In Jesus's darkest moment, the Father's love and faithfulness never wavered.

Jesus was shamed unlike any other so that he could cover our shame with his love and free us to live without shame. Jesus was beaten and broken beyond compare so that he could heal our wounds and restore our souls so that we can love again. What the ending of our stories *should* be, Jesus took for us. Jesus experienced God's just and righteous punishment so that we would be spared God's wrath, making it possible for us to enjoy communion with God. Jesus was forsaken so that he could bring us into his unbreakable covenant of love, assuring us that he will never leave or forsake us.

Jesus "learned obedience from what he suffered and, once made perfect, became the source of eternal salvation for all who obey him" (Hebrews 5:8–9). This does not mean that Jesus turned from disobedience to obedience, but that he lived a sinless life on earth. Through various trials, he demonstrated over and over his absolute trust and obedience to his Father. Through every temptation thrown at him by the devil, he lived with unwavering submission to God. And through each and every hardship, his obedience testified to his perfection so we might see him as the only source of eternal salvation.

We can find comfort knowing that God's love and faithfulness are steadfast in our darkest and most painful times. All Jesus suffered on the cross should convince us that he is our perfect high priest. Only Jesus can fully identify with the injustice, heartache, affliction, sorrow, and trauma we experience in this evil world. Jesus personally understands and relates to our pain in our stories unlike anyone else. Not only does Jesus understand our burdens and brokenness, but he is the only one able to bear our burdens and bind up our brokenness.

How Does Jesus Make a Difference Now?

Emma has struggled to see how Jesus could make a difference in her upside-down world. Her heart has ached with a sense of hopelessness. She has felt helpless and out of control in the face of her infertility and her husband's unfaithfulness. One night, out of sheer desperation, she picked up her Bible and flipped to 2 Peter 1. Her eyes and heart were captured by what she read: "His divine power has given us everything we need for a godly life through our knowledge of him who called us by his own glory and goodness. Through these he has given us his very great and precious promises, so that through them you may participate in the divine nature, having escaped the corruption in the world caused by evil desires" (2 Peter 1:3–4).

In an instant, the Spirit of God helped Emma understand how the Lord had given her divine power to live a godly life—to live in God's *presence* and to find hope in his precious *promises* through Jesus Christ. God was with her in her pain and darkness. His life-giving promises remind her of his faithfulness and goodness. Even though her circumstances had not changed, in that moment, she experienced God's comfort and peace through the power of God.

Don't believe for a moment that your hardships, afflictions, and troubles have the last word. Your fears, anxieties, shame, anger, and sorrow don't have to rule you. Jesus came to be your refuge, your stronghold, and your fortress. He serves as your perfect high priest, advocate, and intercessor.

God's Invitation

Spend some time in God's Word. Open your heart to God and share with him the trials you are facing and how they have impacted you.

Read Isaiah 52:13—53:12 slowly once or twice as you consider your difficulties. Consider the sufferings of Christ for you. Reflect on how his life and death offer hope to you.

CHAPTER 9
REDEMPTION:
WE LIVE IN GOD'S PRESENCE

STEVE HAS struggled with a deep sense of shame and guilt as the reality of his adultery has confronted him. Over the past several months since his conversation at the restaurant with Marcus, he has slowed down enough to reflect on his heart, life, and relationship with God. Day by day God has given him more clarity. Steve has seen more clearly how his and Emma's infertility struggles had taken first place in their lives, and how he had sought relief from the stress and strain. He'd convinced himself that Emma wanted a baby more than she wanted him. As a result, he sought affirmation from another woman, Bella, who gave him the attention he craved and the pleasure he desired.

Our Incurable Condition Will Be Restored

Steve enjoyed reading the Old Testament prophets who spoke of God's absolute power and purpose so forcefully. One evening, as he read how Jeremiah confronted Israel with a relentless call to repentance, he was reminded of his own sinfulness: "This is what the LORD says: 'Your wound is incurable, your injury beyond healing. There is no one to plead your cause, no remedy for your sore, no healing for you. . . . Why do you cry out over your wound, your pain that has no cure? Because of your great guilt and many sins I have done these things to you'" (Jeremiah 30:12–13, 15).

After reading these verses, Steve had started to weep uncontrollably. He had begun to feel the weight of his sins—lying to Emma, betraying her trust, and defiling their marriage bed.

Before, whenever he would hurt Emma with harsh words or impatience, Steve would berate himself, plead with God to change him, and convince Emma that he would do better. But the inevitable would happen, and he would lash out in anger again, pushing Emma further away each time. As his affair with Bella progressed, Steve's shame had convinced him that God would never take him back and that he was not worthy of love. His sin made him feel far away from God. As a result, he sunk into deep despair and hopelessness.

Now God's Spirit was leading Steve to a different perspective, helping him to see that his sins were against and ever before God. He was learning that even his secret sins are exposed in the light of God's presence (Psalm 90:8). God was showing Steve his pride, his self-preoccupation, and the way he has been consumed with a fantasy world where he had been seeking after anything that he thought would satisfy him. What Steve saw most clearly was how he had lived as if God was irrelevant to his thoughts, desires, and purpose. He'd viewed the Bible as mere words on a page, not as God's living Word. He'd never realized before that the Scriptures are a gift from God that reveal God's heart and show us how to live and love. Steve knew he deserved God's discipline, but he also began to see his misery and brokenness as a tool in God's hand. In exposing his sinfulness and calling Steve to repentance, God was being merciful and kind.

As Steve's thoughts turned to his separation from Emma and the current state of their marriage, he recognized that he could not demand Emma's forgiveness nor convince her to reconcile with him. Mending their marriage would be God's work. But in God's presence, Steve was not without hope. As Steve read, "'But I will restore you to health and heal your wounds,' declares the LORD" (Jeremiah 30:17), he felt an immediate sense of peace and comfort. His tears turned to joy, and he was overwhelmed with God's mercy and grace. Steve then read, "So you will be my people, and I will be your God" (v. 22). In spite of all the ways he had sinned against God and Emma, God still loved Steve, and Steve felt it in a way that was undeniable and unexplainable. God's presence was a comfort, and a promise that Steve was not forsaken.

A Struggle for Confidence

Even as Christians, we sometimes lack confidence in our salvation. If we have a chronic sin struggle, for instance, we can question whether or not the Holy Spirit is really working in us. We may also question God when we've pleaded with him to change us or our circumstances and nothing changes. When we doubt like this, we can live defeated lives, convinced we're alone and helpless.

As we saw in chapter 8, working through the painful memories of what had happened to her as a teenager had taken a toll on Nikki. She had struggled with fear and anxiety in ways she never experienced before. Unexpected sounds or smells would trigger memories of that dreadful night, sending her into a state of panic. She used to be a confident, free-spirited young woman, but she had become more and more insecure as the years passed. In her recent return to the Lord, Nikki had become more confident in her relationship with God and she was now getting better sleep, but this didn't translate into every aspect of her life. As more traumatic memories surfaced, doubts plagued her. Nikki just couldn't seem to reconcile God's steadfast love with the fact that he allowed her to be attacked. God seemed so far away from that situation.

The Enemy seeks to undermine our confidence in God's Word and his love. He knows that he can't separate us from God, but he aims to remove any assurance that would enable us to experience God's reassuring love, life-giving joy, and soul-settling peace. Often our difficult realities become our reference point, the filter through which we understand our life and our relationship to God. Obsessive thoughts about life's uncertainties combine with Satan's lies to fuel doubts and despair. We may feel fearful and hopeless, thinking God is distant and uncaring. We may even push God to the side, convinced that we need to take charge of circumstances that seem out of control.

We were never meant to be the center of our world. We weren't created to rely on our own understanding or strength. When doubts and despair put God at a distance, our world becomes more chaotic, and our souls become more disordered. But in our confusion and darkness, God calls us to trust him, fix our eyes on him, and follow him. He is with us as he shepherds us through life's dark valleys.

There is no place we can go where we can escape from his Spirit and flee from his presence (Psalm 139:7–10).

A Needed Shift in Perspective

Nikki was doodling in her journal. She drew a stick figure to represent herself. Above that she wrote the word GOD. Nikki thought of herself in a pit of darkness, looking up at God. She drew a question mark for each of her unanswered questions until question marks covered the page. Then, as she sat staring at her drawing, something shifted within her. She started to imagine her life from God's perspective. She thought about how he had formed her in her mother's womb and ordained all of her days before she was born (Psalm 139:16). If this was true, then he knew her struggles growing up with divorced parents, the sexual assault, her move to America, her difficulties with work and rest, and the countless other details of her life. Nikki then reflected on how God chose to save her before the creation of the world to "be holy and blameless before him in love" (Ephesians 1:4 ESV). God chose her though he knew all of the ugly parts of her story. This fact made her feel known and valued. Nikki realized that God personally sought to redeem her; and that he knew the pain and hardship, fear and shame, and guilt and sorrow of living in a fallen, evil world. As she looks back at her story, she is beginning to see God's presence more clearly throughout her life.

Next Nikki drew a cross between her and God. She considered how the heavenly Father sent his Son to atone for her sins, and she was overwhelmed by his love (1 John 4:9–10). God had forgiven her sins and declared her not guilty through the cross of Christ. That redemption reality brought her into union, into an intimate and inseparable relationship with Jesus (Colossians 1:13–14). Nikki thought about how she now had life in Christ, and how he offers her the comfort she so desperately needs. She considered how God has poured out his love into her heart through the Holy Spirit (Romans 5:5) with the goal of transforming and restoring her soul that had been twisted by sin and traumatized by evil. She imagined how the Spirit of God and Jesus were praying for her (Romans 8:26–27, 34). She not only envisioned it, but she also experienced the light of the world piercing her darkness as Christ's love revived her despondent heart.

Nikki's eyes were drawn back to all the question marks on the page. She realized that her view of God and her relationship with him had been shaped by her story. God's story, revealed through his Word, needed to inform her perspective. As Nikki reflected on who God is and upon his relationship to her, she began to see and experience how God knows her intimately and loves her personally. With a shift in her reference point, she sat back in her chair, took a deep breath, and then exhaled with a sigh of relief. A wave of deep peace washed through her as she accepted how God might not ever answer all of her questions.

Instead of giving her all the answers, she understood that God had given all of *himself* to her. She smiled and said to herself, "I'll settle for that."

Our Struggle with Loneliness

When we lack confidence in God and his presence, we can feel all alone; it is us against the world. Everyone struggles with loneliness at various points in their lives. For some, such struggles are cyclical. For others, feeling lonely is a chronic struggle.

Have you ever been surrounded by people—coworkers, friends, or family—yet you still felt all alone? You might convince yourself you are not alone when engaging with social media "friends." You might feel less lonely when you play video games with teammates across the globe, or cheer on your favorite team from your living room with the fans on TV. You may turn to chat rooms where you pay for conversations or indulge in porn as a way of fantasizing about a gratifying "relationship." You may even commiserate with strangers at the neighborhood pub. But the truth is, the presence of people doesn't diminish loneliness, nor do your fantasies or other forms of escapism. We feel lonely when we lack meaningful relationships. When we're lonely, we feel that we do not belong, are not known, or are not valued or loved. Feeling alone and being alone affects how we see and experience all of life.

Let's consider the effect of loneliness by looking at life from a contrary perspective. Life has more purpose when we love others, and others love us. Heartaches seem more bearable when we can share our struggles with those who care. We experience greater joy when we can celebrate with those who are close to us. Situations seem less scary when someone is by our side, journeying with us. We can wait with more patience and less anxiety during times of uncertainty when others support and encourage us.

God Knows and Addresses Our Loneliness

God knows all of the ways we struggle with loneliness, and he understands how loneliness influences the way we live and love. He knows that we deal with loneliness because of the fall. It's evil that keeps us from experiencing love.

Remember that back in the creation story, God declared that it was not good for us to be alone (Genesis 2:18). God didn't design us to live life by ourselves. He created us for communion with him and fellowship with one another. The two great commandments also reveal God's purpose for us to live in relationship with him and others (Matthew 22:37–40). These commands remind us of our relational priorities. God designed us to depend on him and on others. This relational dependency holds true now and in eternity. In the new heavens and new earth, we will not experience a single moment of loneliness. God's goal in making all things new is for us to experience perfect love through perfect relationships. We will enjoy love with God and others in endless ways.

But what about now, on this side of heaven? Even now God wants us to experience his perfect presence and love. Sometimes we take God's presence for granted, but a look back to the Old Testament will shake us out of our apathy and arrogance. When God gave the Law to Israel at Sinai, he drew near to his people. He told them not to set a foot on the mountain lest they be consumed by fire and die. His presence was powerful, so powerful it was dangerous. Later, when God's presence descended upon the tabernacle, only the high priest could enter the Most Holy Place, and that only once each year! But *now* Jesus gives us an open invitation into his presence. He invites us to approach his throne boldly and confidently, to "receive mercy and find grace to help us in our time of need" (Hebrews 4:16).

We Can Struggle to Trust and Experience God's Presence

Though we still live in a fallen world, Christians live in union with Christ through his Spirit. Though we still struggle with loneliness on this side of heaven, we can know and experience Christ's perfect love right now. One of the gospel's beautiful and comforting realities is that because of your union with Christ, you always live in God's presence. You are never alone. God's presence comes through the indwelling of the Holy Spirit.

In John 14, when Jesus starts telling his disciples of his departure, they are understandably upset. They cannot imagine not having their Lord with them in the same room. But Jesus promises that they will not be alone. God would send his Spirit, the Comforter, who would be with them forever. God's presence would always be with his people.

You may struggle to trust and experience God's presence. After all, God is spirit, so we cannot see, hear, or touch him. Moreover, you may be discouraged and battling despair. These struggles can dull our senses and numb our hearts. Doubts and disobedience can also harden our hearts and keep us from knowing and experiencing God in real and personal ways.

But here is some good news: God leaves no room for doubt about his presence. One of his names is Immanuel, which means "God with us" (Isaiah 7:14; Matthew 1:23). You might say God's presence is everything. You do not need to be a seasoned saint or a committed monk or nun to experience God's abiding presence. You don't have to be flawless to be confident that God is with you. As you look at his story, God's great love for you should assure you that he will never leave you nor forsake you. Jesus created you to live in his presence. He died for you so that you might live through him now and in his presence forever.

God Shepherds Us in His Presence

Emma spends most of her weekends curled up on her sofa or in bed. She wraps her favorite blanket around her, puts on soft instrumental music, and immerses herself in a book. She just wants to numb the pain and loneliness. The other night she read 2 Peter 1 and was reminded that God has given her his divine power and precious promises. This has brought her comfort and a renewed interest in God's Word. She has decided to begin a new journey through the Psalms.

Before, Emma had read the Psalms as a distant observer—thinking of the words of the psalmists as directed at readers in the distant past. But now in this season of desperation and shame, humiliation and heartache, she has found the Psalms to be a way both to voice her heart's cry and to hear God's heart. The Psalms have helped Emma know that God is with her.

One evening while reading the Psalms, Emma senses God inviting her to seek refuge in him. "Keep me safe, my God, for in you I take refuge. I say to the LORD, 'You are my LORD; apart from you I have no good thing'" (Psalm 16:1–2). The word "refuge" gives Emma an image of the safety and strength she longs for. It dawns on her that she's sought refuge in reading. Books take Emma's mind off the millions of anxious thoughts that race through her mind. The characters in the stories distract her from the deep ache in her heart. But God invites Emma to seek refuge in him instead of her books. In the shelter of his presence, God promises to provide the goodness her soul needs.

Emma stops to reflect on Psalm 16:7–10. The psalm reminds her that God counsels her with his wisdom even when she lies in bed at night (v. 7). Emma begins to understand that she needs to "keep her eyes always on the Lord," to be attentive to God and expect him to shepherd her. She reads that he promises to be present with her and not let her be shaken (v. 8). She is amazed that even in her current circumstances—abandoned by her husband and separated from him—her heart can experience gladness. Emma is able to rejoice, and she feels more secure, knowing she can rest in one who will not abandon her (vv. 9–10).

Emma finds her confidence in God growing as she works through the psalm. Though her whole world seems to be falling apart externally, she has been able to sit back, take a deep breath, and rest in Christ as she reads: "You make known to me the path of life; you will fill me with joy in your presence, with eternal pleasures at your right hand" (v. 11).

Emma journals her reflections: "God knows me, protects me, and he'll help me know the way to go next as I follow him." Emma notices that her mind isn't racing into chaos and despair as she brings her circumstances to God. She doesn't have to distract herself to avoid the pain. Instead, she finds herself able to experience God's presence and comfort in her brokenness. Emma comes to understand that two realities can be true at the same time: She can experience God's comfort and love even in the midst of her heartache.

God's Presence Gives Perspective

When you draw near to God and open his Word, he'll clarify your confusion and disperse your doubts (Psalm 73:16–17). His presence reframes how you see your story and struggles. In his presence, God enables you to experience and trust him.

You may feel alone, but the Word reminds you, "Surely I am with you always, to the very end of the age" (Matthew 28:20). Jesus promises, "Never will I leave you; never will I forsake you" (Hebrews 13:5). If you are in Christ, he dwells in you, and you reside in him. Jesus says, "You will realize that I am in my Father, and you are in me, and I am in you" (John 14:20).

God may seem far away, or you may think God is nowhere to be found, but he pursues you with his love: "Surely your goodness and love will follow me all the days of my life" (Psalm 23:6). Jesus invites you to draw near to him, "Come to me, all you who are weary and burdened, and I will give you rest" (Matthew 11:28).

God assures you of his care for you: "He gathers the lambs in his arms and carries them close to his heart; he gently leads those that have young" (Isaiah 40:11). The psalmist says, "The LORD is close to the brokenhearted and saves those who are crushed in spirit" (Psalm 34:18).

As you walk with him, the glory of God's presence will pierce the darkness of your reality and lift your gaze toward him. As you look up, remember that you live in God's bigger reality. As you live in his story and make it your frame of reference, you can know and experience all of the spiritual blessings found in Jesus (Ephesians 1:3).

God's Presence Enables You to Experience His Blessings

You may be skeptical about receiving anything from God. You may have had countless devotional times, but felt nothing. And, as a result, frustration and disappointment have settled deep in your soul. Perhaps your pain, fear, or grief is so overwhelming that it drowns out any other emotional experience, and you feel numb. It may even be that your heart is hardened towards God and you are no longer interested in what he has to offer. Regardless of where you are, God will never give up on you. His love for you never changes. He will never stop pursuing you.

What are some of the spiritual blessings you can experience in Christ right now, even as you live in this fallen world? Take a moment to meditate on the following realities:

- Jesus is the vine, you are united to him as a branch. His life flows through you. "If you remain in me and I in you, you will bear much fruit" (John 15:5). As a result, you can experience his love, joy, and peace (Galatians 5:22).

- God is your Good Shepherd, and he is with you, renewing you: "He makes me lie down in green pastures, he leads me beside still waters. He restores my soul" (Psalm 23:2–3 ESV).

- The God of all comfort is ever-present to comfort you in all your troubles: "Praise be to the God and Father of our Lord Jesus Christ, the Father of compassion and the God of all comfort" (2 Corinthians 1:3). You can say with David, "Even though I walk through the darkest valley, I will fear no evil, for you are with me; your rod and your staff, they comfort me" (Psalm 23:4).

- God invites you to experience his eternal pleasures and the fullness of his joy: "You will fill me with joy in your presence, with eternal pleasures at your right hand" (Psalm 16:11).

- Jesus is whispering to you, "Peace I leave with you; my peace I give you. I do not give to you as the world gives. Do not let your hearts be troubled and do not be afraid. . . . I have told you these things, so that in me you may have peace. In this world you will have trouble. But take heart! I have overcome the world" (John 14:27; 16:33).

God created us for communion with him so that we can taste and see his goodness even in our present difficult circumstances. Living in and experiencing God's presence will change your perspective and the way your live.

God's Presence Protects and Provides

There is nothing more beautiful to dwell upon than the reality that we are in union with Love himself. It's our present experience of this union—our experience of God's presence—that he uses to protect us from dark danger and provide for our deepest needs. The presence of God's perfect love casts out our fear (1 John 4:18) and compels us to live for him rather than for ourselves (2 Corinthians 5:14–15). When we stand and behold the glorious love of God in the face of Christ, we are changed into his image with increasing glory (2 Corinthians 3:18). As we experience God's love, confident that he will take everything that is meant for evil and use it for good, we find rest in life's biggest storms. We can live with confidence and freedom, trusting that our loving God will complete in us the work he began (Philippians 1:6).

God's Invitation

Spend some time with God through his Word. Open your heart to God and share with him how you may struggle with loneliness or how you doubt his presence in your life.

Read Psalm 84 slowly once or twice as you consider your struggles. God invites you to draw near to him and to dwell in his presence.

CHAPTER 10
REDEMPTION: WE LIVE IN GOD'S PROMISES

AT RANDOM times throughout each day, Emma found herself dwelling on Steve's betrayal. What could he have been thinking when he decided to break their marriage vows? Was she not good enough for him? What did the other woman have that she didn't? Emma knew that she and Steve didn't have a perfect marriage. They had their share of struggles. But they were supposed to stand by each other through good times and bad, in sickness and in health. Now Steve had not only been unfaithful, but he'd lied to her when she suspected something was wrong. He'd promised her that nothing was going on, and he'd even reminded her of their marriage vows. What happened? How could she trust him again?

When we sin or are sinned against, it's easy to doubt God. The Enemy seeks to deceive us with the lie that we're not good enough. The world distracts us with promises of satisfaction, comfort, and safety. Our sinful desires lead us to follow our own understanding instead of God's ways. In this relentless spiritual battle, the Enemy leverages the twists and turns and the brokenness and uncertainty of life to discourage us. He fills our hearts and minds with doubts about God's Word and his love. If the doubts linger long enough, our discouragement can lapse into despair, and we can lose all hope. In this downward spiral, God seems more and more distant.

Specifically, we doubt God's promises. We think they don't apply to us. We reject them, because our hearts are bitter and jaded, numb and hardened towards God. We don't think we need what God's promises offer. Or, perhaps, we know God's promises are true but we simply don't want to wait for his plan to unfold.

But, in reality, God's loving promises are exactly what we need. They are life-giving and hope-filled. They are the nutrients our soul needs to flourish.

God's Covenant of Love

Unlike marriage covenants that are broken when expectations aren't met, love diminishes, or someone decides to end the relationship for whatever reason, God's covenants with his people are characterized by loyalty and love.[16] Moses wrote, "Know therefore that the LORD your God is God; he is the faithful God, keeping his *covenant of love* to a thousand generations of those who love him and keep his commandments" (Deuteronomy 7:9; cf. Daniel 9:4). God remembers his covenant forever (1 Chronicles 16:15).

Imagine, the God who made heaven and earth pledged his enduring love and faithfulness to his people. God's pledge will not end with death, but will endure for eternity. His covenant of love does not end when we're unfaithful and fail to love him in return. God will never violate his covenant or alter what he promised. God has sworn by his holiness and will not lie. His covenant is more enduring than the sun and moon (Psalm 89:34–37). About his covenant promises, God says: "I will betroth you to me forever; I will betroth you in righteousness and justice, in love and compassion. I will betroth you in faithfulness, and you will acknowledge the LORD" (Hosea 2:19–20).

Think about the extreme mercy and kindness of God's covenant love. God has promised to love you through good and bad, through sickness and health. He has promised to love you before you ever loved him. When he saved you, he did all he needed to do to ensure that you could never be snatched away from his love (John 10:28). He has rooted and grounded you in his love (Ephesians 3:17). He has poured out his love into your heart through his Spirit (Romans 5:5). He has promised to love you even when you doubt, disobey, or seek after other lovers. He has loved you even when you have accused him of not being faithful. He has loved you even when you have blamed him for the evil you've experienced.

God's covenant of love includes all of his promises declared throughout the Scripture. Every word God speaks is a promise about who he is and what he will do. We can trust God's promises because he never lies (Titus 1:2), and he has the power to accomplish all that he says (Isaiah 55:11).

You may struggle to trust that God's promises are true. You may lack assurance that God's Word addresses your specific needs. You may believe that God's promises address others' realities, but you question whether they apply to you. The Enemy seeks to undermine God's promises. But God's covenant of love is like a fortress within which "neither death nor life, neither angels nor demons, neither the present nor the future, nor any powers, neither height nor depth, nor anything else in all creation will be able to separate us from the love of God that is in Christ Jesus our Lord" (Romans 8:38–39). Neither our sin nor shame can separate us from God's redeeming love.

God's Promises Are "Yes" in Christ

Not only are God's covenants trustworthy and true, but they are further secured through Christ. In 2 Corinthians 1:20–22, the apostle Paul describes Jesus as our Yes and Amen: "For no matter how many promises God has made, they are 'Yes' in Christ. And so through him the 'Amen' ["this is true" or "I agree"] is spoken by us to the glory of God. Now it is God who makes both us and you stand firm in Christ. He anointed us, set his seal of ownership on us, and put his Spirit in our hearts as a deposit, guaranteeing what is to come." God's promises are yes in Christ and guaranteed by the Spirit. You won't find more security and confidence anywhere.

Whenever we say Amen, we give God glory and agree with him that Jesus is the Faithful One who keeps all of God's promises to us from beginning to end. In the Old Testament, God promises a coming Messiah. The Father fulfills this promise when he sends the Son from heaven. Jesus ushers in the kingdom of heaven through his life, death, and resurrection. At the end of God's story, Jesus will ride in on a white horse as the great hero. Revelation 19:11 tells us his name, "Faithful and True." Until that day, God has given us his Spirit as a guarantee that he will keep his promises both now and forever.

God Promises Sweet Communion and Confidence in the Battle

Why are God's promises important? The reason is given to us in 2 Peter 1:3–4: "His divine power has given us everything we need for a godly life through our knowledge of him who called us by his own glory and goodness. Through these he has given us his very great and precious promises, *so that* through them you may participate in the divine nature, having escaped the corruption in the world caused by evil desires" (emphasis mine).

God gives us his divine power and his very great and precious promises so that we can participate in his divine nature. What does this mean?

First, God gives us his promises so that we can commune with the Father, Son, and Holy Spirit. Christians are not absorbed into God's deity; we don't literally become divine. But, because we have been united to Christ and have received the Holy Spirit, we are God's children (John 1:12; Romans 8:9–21). As we dwell in God's presence and behold his beauty, he changes us into the image of Christ. God not only wants us to live with him and to live for him, but he also wants us to live like him. Even though we have already inherited God's promises when we come to faith, we can only experience a partial fulfillment of them on this side of heaven.

Second, in giving us his promises, God helps us to escape this world's corruption. The Holy Spirit changes our evil desires into godly desires. This doesn't mean we've fully escaped the fallen world. Christians still sin and experience the world's brokenness. But we have God's very great and precious promises to keep us even as we struggle with our own evil desires and are sinned against by others.

We may doubt God's goodness, but these doubts do not negate the reality and truth of his character. However, doubts do keep us from knowing and experiencing all that God promises in its fullness. In fact, Paul describes the entire Christian life as a battle against doubt, a "fight of faith" (1 Timothy 6:12). When we doubt, we lower the shield of faith. As a result, we take more direct hits from the "flaming arrows of the evil one" (Ephesians 6:16). God protects us when we trust him. Hear this encouragement from David: "The LORD's unfailing love surrounds the one who trusts in him" (Psalm 32:10). Let us look to Christ and rehearse God's promises. Then, he will be our reference and refuge.

God's Promises Point Us to Christ and Encourage Us to Live Differently

God knows that your struggles can entangle and enslave you, filling your hearts with obsessive thoughts, escalating emotions, and evil desires. Your persistent and painful realities can also redirect your gaze from Christ to your circumstances. It's what captures your heart that determines the way you live (Philippians 4:8). When you fix your eyes on the realities below the "clouds" (see the diagram in chapter 3), this world's corruption shapes how you live and love more than Christ's love and glory. Our stories tend to be shaped by what we do and experience, not by what God's story can and will do. But God's promises remind us of what is true by pointing us to Christ. This gives us hope and courage to live differently.

In 2 Corinthians 6, Paul reminds the Corinthians about God's promise to live with them, make them holy, and welcome them into his family (vv. 6, 16–18). Paul concludes, "Therefore, since we have these promises, dear friends, let us purify ourselves from everything that contaminates body and spirit, perfecting holiness out of reverence for God" (2 Corinthians 7:1). God's promises comfort us during our times of need and reorient us in our confusion. But God's promise of every spiritual blessing in Christ also compels us to purify ourselves from the evil that has defiled our bodies and souls. His promises prompt us to work out our salvation. They also free us to live for God and to love others as he first loved us. Peter spells out this progression, "Now that you have purified yourselves by obeying the truth so that you have sincere love for each other, love one another deeply, from the heart" (1 Peter 1:22).

There is an undeniable connection between what we know to be true (God's trustworthy promises) and how we live out this truth (purifying ourselves). What we believe drives how we live and love. Specifically, God's promises give us hope and compel us to obey his commands to love him and to love others (John 14:15; 15:10).

But what are the promises that give us confidence for spiritual battle? What are the promises that point us to Christ and encourage us to live differently? Let's take a look at three:

God Promises to Never Leave You Nor Forget You

One of Emma's greatest fears is being alone. After Steve left her, she had to face her infertility and the fact that he'd abandoned her for another woman. Emma was by herself.

This intensified her fear and the pain of her loneliness. In her dark moments, she felt forgotten. The heartache seemed unbearable, and the sense of isolation felt unnatural.

In these moments, God reminded Emma of his promise to never leave her. He made his presence known to her in subtle yet sweet ways. One day, Emma sat alone reading her Bible in the dreaded silence of her house. As she read, she wrote down her reflections, and while she was writing, Emma heard the birds chirping outside her window. The birds' presence reminded her of the One who had created them. In that moment, she turned to Deuteronomy 31, one of the assigned Scripture passages for the day in her reading plan. She read, "Be strong and courageous. Do not be afraid or terrified because of them, for the LORD your God goes with you; he will never leave you nor forsake you" (Deuteronomy 31:6). The comfort of God's presence flowed over Emma as she was assured of God's promise to be present even in her fear and sorrow.

The next passage in her reading plan was in Isaiah. Emma was surprised to find how her life paralleled that of the Israelites. They complained that God had forgotten them in their troubles. Then, Emma read God's response, "Can a woman forget her nursing child, that she should have no compassion on the son of her womb? Even these may forget, yet I will not forget you. Behold, I have engraved you on the palms of my hands" (Isaiah 49:15–16 ESV). Emma sat silently, and she received all that God was saying to her. She was amazed by how God spoke directly to her greatest fear through his Word. His story promised that he would not forget her in her pain and darkness. God's promise also soothed the sorrow related to her infertility.

Jesus is perfect love, so you can live without fear in his presence. Jesus is the Man of Sorrows and acquainted with grief. He bore your grief and sorrow (Isaiah 53:3–4 ESV). So, as you live in Christ, you can live with hope and rejoice in your salvation even in the midst of searing loss.

God Promises That Nothing Can Separate You from His Love

Nikki sinks into despair, dwelling again on that fateful night as a teenager. In her shame, she feels worthless and unlovable. She's overcome with guilt and regret, "Why did I go to that party? Why did I get into the car with a guy I had known for less than an hour?" The onslaught of recurring flashbacks convince Nikki that she'll never be able to escape traumatic memories.

But in these dark moments, Nikki also cries out to God, hoping somehow that Christ can offer relief from her shame and guilt. She opens her Bible to Romans 8. This chapter has become a dear friend. Just a few weeks back, God used this passage to remind Nikki that she is not alone in her struggles. Reading God's promise that both the Son and the Spirit pray for her without ceasing brought her comfort (Romans 8:26–27, 34).

Now, as she opens to Romans 8 again, she is overwhelmed by God's promised love:

> Who shall separate us from the love of Christ? Shall trouble or hardship or persecution or famine or nakedness or danger or sword? . . . No, in all these things we are more than conquerors through him who loved us. For I am convinced that neither death nor life, neither angels nor demons, neither

the present nor the future, nor any powers, neither height nor depth, nor anything else in all creation, will be able to separate us from the love of God that is in Christ Jesus our Lord. Romans 8:35, 37–39

Nikki sits, reads, and allows God's promise to soak in. As she does, the weight of her shame and guilt lifts. She feels loved and valued by her God as she considers how no guilt or shame can separate her from the love of her victorious Savior.

God Promises That His Love Is Better Than Life

Mark looked forward to his post-work commute when he would spend time reading and reflecting on God's Word. He was experiencing God through his Word in ways he never had before. Now his after-work commute was something he looked forward to. God's promises seemed to jump off the Bible's pages as he read.

Mark has experienced growth in his struggle with pornography, but now recognizes other ways he escapes into fantasy to provide comfort and diversion. God has been revealing Mark's heart to him in ways that have humbled and convicted him. Mark has begun to see that his response to feeling lonely or discontented has been to immediately reach out to friends for help, read self-help books to find insight, eat and drink for comfort, or play video games as a means of escape. None of these things is inherently wrong, but Mark has realized he has sought these things more often than he sought refuge in God. Mark acknowledged a real struggle with fantasy. He now is seeing that he tends to run away from reality in order to escape life's difficulties or to satisfy his heart's longings.

Then, during one afternoon commute, Mark read: "Because your love is better than life, my lips will glorify you. I will praise you as long as I live, and in your name I will lift up my hands. I will be fully satisfied as with the richest of foods; with singing lips my mouth will praise you" (Psalm 63:3–5).

God has used his promises in this psalm to shift Mark's perspective, to point him to Christ, to give him hope, and to invite him to live differently. Mark knew that good food satisfied him and that he'd found pleasure in porn. But he also knew that both only offered temporary pleasure. When he overindulged in food, he would feel uncomfortably bloated and regret his lack of self-control. When he was lonely or disenchanted and turned to pornography, he would experience shame and guilt, sometimes to the point of self-hatred.

Mark wondered if what he read in Psalm 63 could be true. Could God really satisfy him more than food or sexual pleasure? Mark then bowed his head and prayed, "God, will you satisfy me with your love in such a way that I can declare with confidence like David, 'Your love is better than life'?" In that moment, Mark experienced God's tender love and a confidence that Christ offers the ultimate satisfaction and pleasure that his soul was yearning for. Mark prayed that God's love would compel him to no longer live for himself but rather to live for Jesus Christ (2 Corinthians 5:14–15).

God's Promises Get Better with Age

Just as the flavor and aroma of wine gets more pleasing with age, God's promises also take on a richer meaning and purpose as we walk with Christ over years. Our stories within God's story get deeper as we go. God's promises never change, but they can yield different riches and offer deeper comfort as we understand and apply them again and again through the changing seasons of our lives. Regardless of our age, God promises to provide mercy and grace in our time of need. God's promises have been thoroughly tested throughout his story (Psalm 119:140), so we can be confident as we recall them again and again.

God's Invitation

Spend some time with God through his Word. Open your heart to God and share with him which of his promises you struggle to believe for yourself.

Read Psalm 103 slowly once or twice as you consider your struggle to trust him and others. Look for God's promises and listen to how he is speaking to you through this passage.

CHAPTER 11
REDEMPTION: WE LIVE IN GOD'S POWER

DECEMBER WAS coming to an end, and Mark had decided to use a long holiday weekend to reflect on everything he had experienced over the past year. He went through his calendar and his journal so that he could capture some highlights of the past twelve months. Mark first reflected back to the beginning of the year. In January and February, he had been doing all he could to survive the monotonous routine of life. Mark had felt purposeless; he'd go to work and come home feeling lonely and unwanted. He'd ended every day escaping through video games or pornography. He also struggled with why his biological parents didn't want him.

In the spring, Mark had begun his personal history project, mapping out significant life experiences. He had soon seen that loneliness and being unwanted were themes in his story. Mark also understood how these themes shaped how he related and responded to others, including God. And he had seen a pattern in the ways he'd responded to the two themes. The video games and porn were ways of trying to escape his sense of sorrow and shame. Ultimately,

Mark knew he was accountable for these sinful attempts at escape.

By the summertime, it had been clear that God was changing him. Something remarkable had happened when Mark began to see that the themes of his story didn't define all of reality. As Mark had begun to explore God's story, he had seen the world from a new, bigger frame of reference—one that was much bigger than his little life. Through the summer, God's story had shaped Mark's perspective, and he had begun to understand his identity and purpose from God's perspective. Mark had found hope and meaning when he had learned that God created him for communion. Looking back, Mark could see that he was living more and more "above the clouds." God was shifting both his gaze and his heart.

In September, his journal entries were more frequent. Mark was regularly abiding with Christ during his afternoon train commute. As he read and reflected, Mark had been learning to listen to God's heart through his Word, and he had begun to experience God's love, peace, and comfort. He had been able to fully—with his heart, mind, soul, and strength—experience his relationship with God. Mark had sat back, smiled, and given the Lord thanks.

As the end of the year approached, life had been hard. Work had been demanding, with threats of layoffs. Mark had fractured his wrist in a mountain biking accident. A girl he'd dated had broken up with him. Mark recalled the anxiety of not knowing whether he would have a job, the months of pain and physical therapy for his wrist, and the heartache of the breakup. But as he reflected on these trials, he also saw how God had sustained him. He wasn't turning to fantasy as an escape. Mark couldn't have endured these trials on his own power, but with God's power he could.

Mark has been more comfortable with who he is as a person and where he is at in life. What has helped is knowing that God created him in his image, how evil has impacted him, and how Christ makes a difference as he seeks to live and love. Knowing God's story has given meaning to these parts of his life. He could see how God had been changing and maturing him through life's challenges.

We All Face Limitations and Brokenness

Sometimes we exhaust ourselves to perform, get ahead, and prove we're good enough. But it doesn't take long for life to expose our limitations. Even though we may push ourselves to persevere through tough seasons, everyone has a breaking point. Each of us comes to the place where we are forced to admit we can't do anything more. In his kindness and mercy, God shows us that we are not in control.

But at the same time, you should also understand that while you are not limitless, you are in control of how you relate and respond to the people and situations you encounter. After you've become aware of your limits and acknowledged them to yourself and others, what do you do about them?

Not only do we face limits as finite human beings, but we also encounter the ways that evil has defiled and distorted God's creation. Things are not what they are supposed to be. The longer you live, the more you become aware of how brokenness due to evil exists both within and around you. All people are exposed to evil in the world and thus experience common struggles (chapter 1) like guilt, shame, fear, anger, sorrow, and temptation toward fantasy. But the common struggles aren't merely responses to evil outside of you. They can also flow from your own evil thoughts, emotions, desires, and actions. God tells us that we all plant wickedness, reap evil, and eat the fruit of deception when we depend on human strength instead of on him (Hosea 10:13).

In a fallen world, broken relationships are not the exception. You likely see brokenness in the ways you relate to your family, friends, and coworkers. Consider how you struggle with "bitterness, rage, anger, harsh words, and slander" (Ephesians 4:31 NLT). Think about how you want to please other people to win their favor or how you struggle with insecurity when talking to others. You see such relational brokenness in yourself and others every day.

Our most significant broken relationship is with God. We struggle with doubts about God, and we experience distance from him. Our broken relationship with God impacts our entire life. If we don't relate to God in healthy ways, we won't relate to others in healthy ways. If we don't receive God's love and respond by loving him with all of our heart, soul, mind, and strength, we are incapable of loving others in a God-honoring way. And if our ways of living and loving are broken, the troubles of this world will crush and drown us in despair.

God gave you limitations. He didn't create you to conquer the world. But neither does he call you to merely survive. God knows all the ways you struggle with brokenness. He didn't create you to live a stoic life or to fix yourself. But neither does he call you to live a powerless life.

Empowered by God's Spirit

How does Jesus make a difference in a broken world? In our limits and brokenness, we need to look up and remember that Jesus didn't leave us to take care of ourselves. Instead of letting our reality define what we think is true and doable, God invites us to see life from his perspective. God's story reminds us that he knew all the days of our life and all the troubles we would experience before we were born. Your brokenness is no surprise to God.

God sent his Son to deal with your broken relationship with him. He sent Jesus on a mission to restore your heart and relationships from the brokenness caused by evil. God knows that evil is more powerful than you. He knows you can't survive, let alone thrive, in this world apart from his presence, promises, and power. So, when God saved you, he brought you into union with Christ, the One who created the universe and holds all things together. God also placed his Spirit within you, giving you continuous access to his power. God now invites you to abide in Christ. Jesus spoke directly to your need to draw near to him in desperate dependence. He said, "I am the vine; you are the branches. Whoever abides in me and I in him, he it is that bears much fruit, for apart from me you can do nothing" (John 15:5 ESV). *We tap into God's power by abiding in Christ.*

Your union with Jesus Christ is not merely a theological concept but a life-giving reality to be known and experienced. God's power is not a fantastical superhero power found only in comic books, but a supernatural reality that every believer can experience daily: "For the Kingdom of God is not just a lot of talk; it is living by God's power"

(1 Corinthians 4:20 NLT). God's power is his gift that guarantees his presence and promises, even in your weakness.

Empowered in Your Weakness

Over the last twelve months, God has made Mark more aware of his weakness. Formerly, Mark would have avoided any thought or display of weakness, but putting up a front and trying to pretend he wasn't weak had exhausted him. Moreover, Mark was now more aware of the power he had been given in Christ. He had a growing confidence, not in his own strength, but in Jesus.

Mark had spent the summer reading through the Gospels. Mark had seen how Jesus had lived through the difficulties of a fallen world, experiencing all the pain, testing, and temptation we face because of the fall. But Jesus lived with power as he carried out his mission. He walked in communion with his Father, and he was directed and empowered by God's Spirit. Mark had been blown away by the parallels he saw between Jesus's life and the life God had called him to live in Christ.

Now as the year came to a close, Mark read 2 Corinthians 13: "For to be sure, [Christ] was crucified in weakness, yet he lives by God's power. Likewise, we are weak in him, yet by God's power we will live with him" (v. 4). It encouraged Mark to think that he could live with power like Christ in spite of his weaknesses. He did not need to rely on his own strength but upon God's power, which had been freely given to him. Mark had been freed from his chronic struggle with pornography through the power of God's Spirit dwelling in him.

Mark also took to heart a command in 2 Corinthians 12:9–10. There Paul boasts about his weakness. Mark has clung to this passage as a prayer of hope and help in his ever-present weakness, "God, help me to trust that your grace is sufficient for me as I struggle with loneliness and lust. Please help me to believe that your power is made perfect in my weakness. Please give me the grace to boast all the more gladly about my weaknesses so that your power may rest on me. I want to learn how to delight in you in the midst of temptations, insecurities, hardships, and difficulties. When I am weak, you are strong. Amen."

God invites you to know Christ in your struggles and to experience the power of his resurrected life even during life's storms. As you draw near and hold fast to Jesus, you can fellowship with him, and God will conform you more and more to Christ's image even in the midst of your suffering. You see, God takes what is meant for evil and uses it for good. You can know that God's power is coursing through your soul as you experience contentment in your weakness, confidence in your hardships, and comfort in the midst of chaos.

God strengthens us as we abide in his presence: "For the eyes of the LORD range throughout the earth to strengthen those whose hearts are fully committed to him" (2 Chronicles 16:9). God also empowers us to cling to his promises so that we can trust and obey him when it feels impossible. With the Holy Spirit's help (Romans 8:26), you can live with God's power in at least two distinct ways: (1) by knowing and experiencing his love, and (2) by bearing the fruit of good works.

Empowered to Know and Experience His Love

Emma's time reading the Word and learning to abide in Christ have been life-giving. God's promises have spoken directly to her fear of always being alone. In spite of times of sweet communion, however, her struggles haven't been eliminated. When living by her selfish, sinful *flesh,* she'll convince herself that she can never forgive Steve or love him again given what he did to her. If she's listening to the voices of the *world*—mainly coworkers or talk shows— she's tempted to believe the repeated message that she deserves to be happy and should only look out for herself. The *devil* also attacks Emma. He's seeking to undermine her relationship with God, tempting her to doubt God's love and his Word. If she listens to his lies, Emma can be convinced that God doesn't care for her, that he can't offer what she really needs, and that she should take control of her own life.

The good news is that the tactics of this evil trinity— the flesh, the world, and the devil—consist of mind games and smoke screens. Nothing this trio can throw at Emma can hold up to the power, promises, and presence of God.

In her pain, Emma had obsessed about all the ways Steve had hurt her, and she had become blind to all the ways she had sinned as well. Emma saw Steve as an enemy and a monster. In her self-righteousness, she'd declared, "I could never do the things to Steve that he did to me." But when Emma had turned back to God's Word, God began to show her how she had been sinning against him.

Emma's reading plan took her to the book of Romans. There, she saw that she and Steve are both equally sinners (Romans 3:23) and that the same Savior had shown his grace to both of them (Romans 5:8). Emma was also reminded that it is God's kindness and love that leads us to repentance (Romans 2:4). As she had pondered all that God was showing her, she felt both convicted and loved.

Then Emma received an email from Steve. Her heart sank when she saw it in her inbox; she felt nauseous. It had been several weeks since he'd tried to call her to let her know that he wanted to fight for their marriage. At that time, she couldn't talk with him; he had hurt her too deeply.

Even now, Emma waited until after dinner to read what Steve had sent. She asked the Lord to give her strength and peace, but she felt her anxiety skyrocket. She had to remind herself that God's love was faithful, and his presence was with her. He would give her the power to respond rightly to whatever was in this email. Emma took a deep breath and opened it. As she read Steve's words, she could hear the heart of the man with whom she had fallen in love. Tears began to stream down her face. Steve's words were intentional, and his confession was clear. He owned all that she had known about and suspected. He acknowledged ways he had deceived her, shattered her trust, and crushed her heart.

Steve also reflected on what had been going on in his heart. Steve said that he had come to know and experience God's love in a deep and personal way. As a result, he now believes that God is the only one who can satisfy his deep longings. He understands that no woman, experience, or amount of money can offer the peace and contentment that he yearns for in his soul. As Steve described his struggles, Emma realized that she had never heard Steve talk this way before. She even found herself resonating with some of the same heart struggles as Steve—though she was coming from a different place, because she had been the one sinned against.

Near the end of the email, Steve asked to talk with Emma and hear from her directly about how he had hurt her. Steve explained that he wanted to understand how he had caused her pain and anguish so that he could more fully confess his sins and ask for her forgiveness. Steve then ended his email by saying: "God knows our future and will direct our steps. I know that I don't deserve you or your forgiveness. I know it will take time for you to see that my change of heart and life is God's work and not a scheme to get you back. But regardless of the outcome, I love you and I want God's best for you."

Emma closed her laptop. She didn't know what to think or feel. She'd already reached the point where divorce seemed like her next step. She had started to imagine how her life was going to be different and what needed to change. In one sense, divorce seemed easier and less painful than trying to work things out with a man she didn't trust. She had no guarantees that he wouldn't abandon her again, and she didn't think she could survive another devastating betrayal. Her own power couldn't keep her secure. Oddly, after reading Steve's email, she experienced God's peace and love, which made her feel safe despite the uncertainty of the future.

God's power enables you "to grasp how wide and long and high and deep is the love of Christ, and to know this love that surpasses knowledge—that you may be filled to the measure of all the fullness of God" (Ephesians 3:18–19). God's love anchors you in the storms of life. It guides you along right paths that lead you out of darkness to light. Knowing and experiencing his love shapes what you live for and how you love. His love also compels you to turn to him in repentance so that you no longer live for yourself.

God's Power Bears Fruit

As we abide in the love of Christ, living *with* and *for* God, the Spirit empowers us to bear fruit: "love, joy, peace, patience, kindness, goodness, faithfulness, gentleness, self-control" (Galatians 5:22–23 ESV). Such fruit helps us to thrive even in the worst of times.

Have you witnessed peace and joy in a loved one who is facing a terminal illness? Have you talked with a quadriplegic who not only endures with hope, but also proclaims the hope found in Jesus in the face of decades of excruciating chronic pain? Have you seen the kind of undeniable peace that empowers a person to give thanks to God even when their marriage is not what they dreamed of or when their child goes astray? Such fruit is an amazing gift!

It's not something that can be achieved or earned. No, God created and redeemed all of his people to enjoy a fruitful life through abiding in Christ—through receiving, praying, and living his Word in the power of the Spirit. As we abide in Christ, God's power changes our thoughts, emotions, and desires. He deepens our faith, fuels our hope, and compels us by his love to live for him and not for ourselves.

Two weeks passed after Emma read Steve's email. She had mixed emotions and conflicting thoughts about how to respond. The Psalms gave her comfort and hope during this time. As she read, God reminded her of his faithfulness and nearness. She still felt weak and vulnerable, but God was grounding her in his love with each passing day. Emma decided to open up the book of Ephesians, because she remembered that it had a section about marriage. Oddly enough, God used other sections of the book to encourage and convict her.

Emma longed for a child of her own and a marriage that had not been defiled by adultery, but God reminded her through Ephesians that he had blessed her with every spiritual blessing in Christ (1:3). Emma struggled with letting go of the illusion that she was better than Steve, which offered some relief from her shame. Then, when she saw this self-righteous response for what it was, she felt overwhelmed. She found herself wondering how God would give her the strength to talk with Steve, let alone take steps towards reconciliation. Then, Emma reflected on the reality that God chose her "before the creation of the world to be holy and blameless" (1:4). God showed her that the same power that raised Jesus from the dead is at work in her (1:19–21). Emma spent a couple of hours reading, praying, and journaling these reflections. Then, she went to bed exhausted.

The next morning, Emma called her friend Alice to tell her about Steve's email and invite her over for lunch. She asked Alice if she'd stay the afternoon to read with her and talk about the book of Ephesians. Emma knew that she would benefit from having a trusted friend walk with her as she sought God's wisdom.

That afternoon, Emma shared with Alice how, before the affair, she had viewed Steve as her equal. After his betrayal, however, she saw him as different from her. "Steve broke his wedding vows," said Emma. "He broke our union. We're not one anymore."

"But how does that square with what we just read in Ephesians," asked Alice. The two friends had just read Ephesians 4:4–6: "There is one body and one Spirit . . . one hope . . . one Lord, one faith, one baptism; one God and Father of all, who is over all and through all and in all."

"If Steve and I are both Christians, then we are united as part of Christ's body," answered Emma.

"That's right, you share the same Spirit, hope, Lord, faith, and heavenly Father."

The two friends paused, grabbed a snack, and then continued to work through Ephesians 4. Emma read the final two verses: "Get rid of all bitterness, rage and anger, brawling and slander, along with every form of malice. Be kind and compassionate to one another, forgiving each other, just as in Christ God forgave you" (Ephesians 4:31–32).

Emma was quiet and reached for a tissue. Alice thought she understood why Emma responded to this passage with tears, but she didn't want to assume, so she asked, "What's going on in your heart behind your tears?"

In a shaky voice, Emma answered, "I see the ugliness of my heart. And, at the same time, I feel comforted by the compassion of God's heart. I don't know if I have the desire or strength to forgive Steve."

As soon as that sentence was out of her mouth, Emma's eyes looked ahead to the beginning of the next chapter: "Follow God's example, therefore, as dearly loved children and walk in the way of love, just as Christ loved us and gave himself up for us as a fragrant offering and sacrifice to God" (Ephesians 5:1–2).

Emma and Alice spent the rest of Saturday evening working through what forgiveness means. They wrestled with how forgiveness and love are related. Alice turned to 1 Corinthians 13, and she read God's description of love: "Love is patient, love is kind. It does not envy, it does not boast, it is not proud. It does not dishonor others, it is not self-seeking, it is not easily angered, it keeps no record of wrongs" (13:4–5).

The phrase love "keeps no record of wrongs" caught Emma's attention. "It's so clear that God's love and forgiveness are connected," she said out loud.

At that moment, Alice shared with Emma a passage she had memorized years ago, "For as high as the heavens are above the earth, so great is his love for those who fear him; as far as the east is from the west, so far has he removed our transgressions from us" (Psalm 103:11–12). Both Alice and Emma discussed how God's vast love and forgiveness applied to their own lives.

The Spirit of God was working in Emma in mighty ways, producing in her his love and peace amid her pain. The Lord was cultivating a faithfulness that was moving her towards love and forgiveness, just as Christ had loved and forgiven her. Even Emma was shocked at how God was giving her patience and self-control as she processed Steve's email. She found herself grateful for how God was shepherding her.

Why Jesus Matters in a Broken World

You can live and love differently when you seek refuge in God's presence, find hope in his promises, and are restored through God's power. Regardless of what you have experienced, what you are facing, or what you anticipate in the future, you can be confident when you abide in Christ. You can overcome whatever adversity you face because Jesus has overcome the world (John 16:33; 1 John 4:4). You can conquer whatever has defeated you because you follow the victorious one (2 Corinthians 2:14; Romans 8:37). You can be set free from whatever has kept you in bondage because Jesus is your deliverer (Galatians 5:1; Psalm 34:7). God's power protects you from the schemes of the Enemy through your faith in Jesus Christ (1 Peter 1:5).

When you live in the light of God's story, he gives you his power not only to live a godly life (2 Peter 1:3), but also to participate in his mission. Remember, God created you for love and restored you with his love so that you can love your neighbor in the church and world. "May the God of hope fill you with all joy and peace as you trust in him, so that you may overflow with hope by the power of the Holy Spirit" (Romans 15:13).

God's Invitation

Spend some time in God's Word. Open your heart to God and share with him your insecurities and weaknesses. Or you can share any doubts you may have about his power in your life.

Read Psalm 46 slowly once or twice as you keep in mind what you shared. Look for evidence of God's power and listen to how he is speaking to you through this passage.

CHAPTER 12
CONSUMMATION:
WE WILL ENJOY LOVE
FOREVER

SOME STORIES seem endless. They can be so boring or bad that you want them to stop before they are over. Sadly, the same can be true for your own story. If you are struggling with thinking life is meaningless or not worth living, God is inviting you to look up and find meaning and hope in him. God's love story is beautiful. He wants to *reframe* how you see yourself and your life from his perspective. Though your soul has been severely impacted by evil, he wants to *restore* it as you abide in Christ. Whether you believe it or not, he is *redeeming* the heartache and trauma in *your* story as you live in *his* story. Don't allow life below the clouds or the Enemy's schemes to convince you that God's story is irrelevant. He speaks directly to your present realities and your past experiences. And don't dismiss the end of God's story. Though you may feel hopeless and the end may seem far away, Jesus is coming to make all things new.

How Long, O Lord?

Your story may have left you exhausted and weary. You may have avoided or minimized the hard parts of life through fantasy and escape. Perhaps guilt, regrets, and self-condemnation have stolen your joy, conditioning you to question everything you do and think. Maybe shame has been a constant companion, convincing you that no one would love you if they knew the uniquely dark parts of your story. Perhaps fear, anxiety, and worry have led you to obsess over every possible scenario. Do you think this is the only way to feel a sense of safety and control? Has anger hardened your heart and hurt those around you? Are you overwhelmed with grief and sorrow over something or someone important that has been taken away? Or have you experienced injustice and oppression at the hands of others? All these common struggles you experience in this fallen world may tempt you to give up. You may even experience despair and depression, convinced that nothing will change regardless of what you do.

In addition to common struggles, we all face relational struggles. Relationships can be difficult, unpredictable, and hurtful beyond compare. We long for mutual relationships instead of one-sided neediness. We desire life-giving friendship, not life-draining conversations that only rehash the same issues or turn into arguments when one or both parties escalate or shut down. We wish for encouraging, not discouraging companions. We don't want relationships that are filled with drama, gossip, or self-pity. Sadly, broken hearts and division are everywhere. Expectations end in disappointment. Conflict abounds.

Behind the veil of our common struggles and relational struggles there is the daily skirmish of spiritual warfare. The Enemy schemes against God's people. He deceives us into believing we can find hope, joy, and pleasure apart from God. We believe lies about God, about ourselves, and about others. As a result, we see every aspect of our lives through a distorted lens. The Enemy also distracts us. Often, we're focused on our own realities and cannot see above the clouds to the God who created and redeemed us. In spite of our best efforts to know and experience God, the Enemy still discourages us. And through our struggles with doubts, questions, and anger, he divides us, keeping us from deep intimacy with God and others. We're left alone, bitter, and disillusioned about love—pulling away from God and others in hurt, distrust, and self-protection.

Under the cloud of spiritual warfare, we also encounter faith struggles. Ongoing sin and suffering can drain our faith and fill us with doubts. The deep anguish in our souls can even cause our hearts to sink into despair. Our broken bodies and souls draw our eyes downward and inward, creating distance with God and others.

King David had the same experience. He asked, "How long, LORD? Will you forget me forever? How long will you hide your face from me? How long must I wrestle with my thoughts and day after day have sorrow in my heart? How long will my enemy triumph over me?" (Psalm 13:1–2). Our common struggles, our relational struggles, our faith struggles, and the devil's schemes can feel like the controlling framework for our lives. But these battles are temporary moments in God's story. For David, his struggles led to deeper trust in God and a deeper experience of God's love and glory.

Evil Doesn't Have the Final Word

Jesus sees you in the dark valley, and he sees the dark places of your heart. He knows you are weary and weighed down by your burdens. You may still be struggling to understand how Jesus makes a difference as you live on this side of heaven. But in spite of the troubles you face, setting your gaze on God's entire story makes all the difference in how you see and experience your present struggles and past pain. This is the good news. Even though the fall is part of God's story, it is not the end of the story. God, who is the author of this divine love story, has already written and revealed the story's ending. In God's story, evil doesn't have the last say. Its days are coming to an end.

The end of God's story brings the fulfillment of Jesus's prayer, "Your kingdom come, your will be done, on earth as it is in heaven" (Matthew 6:10). In the book of Revelation, we find heavenly visions, prophetic warnings, a battle between good and evil, and a gloriously intimate picture of the ultimate wedding. When we read the final chapters of God's story, we long for the comfort that is to come in the new heavens and new earth: "He will wipe every tear from their eyes. There will be no more death or mourning or crying or pain, for the old order of things has passed away. He who was seated on the throne said, 'I am making everything new!' Then he said, 'Write this down, for these words are trustworthy and true'" (Revelation 21:4–5).

Imagine living where there is no more harm, no more sickness, no more danger, and no more death. Imagine a perfect peace where there are no stressors within you or around you. Evil will no longer be present in God's kingdom. "Nothing impure will ever enter it, nor will anyone who does what is shameful or deceitful" (Revelation 21:27). God will not only wipe away every tear, but he will wipe away every thought tied to your tears—the sorrow of loss, the misery of suffering, and the chaos of uncertainty.

Imagine what it will be like for the Enemy to no longer be present to whisper destructive lies and deceitful promises that are dangerous and empty. Satan will no longer tempt you to doubt God, draw you into despair, or trick you into believing that God is distant and uncaring. With sin's power defeated, evil will no longer overwhelm or overcome you. All of God's people will follow Jesus in victory for all of eternity.

The devil will not have the final word because he will be locked away in his final resting place, never to be heard again. What will happen to the devil at the end of God's story? The devil and all of his demons, along with death and Hades, will be thrown into the lake of fire, where they "will be tormented day and night for ever and ever" (Revelation 20:10). The forces of evil, along with the sinful and wicked effects of sin, will suffer eternal punishment and damnation. And "anyone whose name [is] not found written in the book of life [will be] thrown into the lake of fire" (Revelation 20:15). In the new heavens and earth, the absence of evil will allow us to know and experience God's love in all of its glorious fullness.

A World of Love

We should not merely understand paradise in terms of what will be absent. It is good news that "no longer will there be any curse" (Revelation 22:3a), but the essence of heaven is found in what will be present: "The throne of God and of the Lamb will be in the city, and his servants will serve him. They will see his face, and his name will be on their foreheads. There will be no more night. They will not need the light of a lamp or the light of the sun, for the

Lord God will give them light. And they will reign for ever and ever" (Revelation 22:3b–5).

We will be in the very presence of Love, seeing the face of God. The glory radiating from the Light of the World will be so majestic and brilliant that there will be no more darkness, nor will there be a need for the light of the sun and moon (Isaiah 60:19–20; Revelation 21:23).

Nikki reflected on heaven, and she found herself in awe as her imagination catapulted her into another world. She envisioned being in the presence of the "Father of compassion and God of all comfort" (2 Corinthians 1:3). In that moment, she felt God's love and mercy wash over her. She felt embraced by his strong presence, and she imagined God the Father's tender voice saying to her, "Well done, good and faithful servant!" (Matthew 25:21). She imagined her Father's delight in her as he rejoiced over her, and all of his people, with singing (Zephaniah 3:17).

As Nikki thought about being in the presence of the Son of God, her Good Shepherd, she could see the warmth of his eyes and love expressed in his face. Abiding in Christ would no longer be a merely spiritual endeavor. Instead, she would be able to dwell in his physical presence. She envisioned how being in the presence of infinite joy would restore her soul once and for all from the evil and wickedness she has seen and experienced. Then, Nikki read another passage about the new heavens and new earth, and it left her speechless: "The former things will not be remembered, nor will they come to mind" (Isaiah 65:17). Nikki was overwhelmed with God's peace as she tried to imagine a life where she will be set free from horrific memories and the emotions that resulted from her past trauma.

Finally, Nikki thought about the Holy Spirit, and pondered how he would empower her to experience God's rich and timeless love—the love that the Father, Son, and Spirit had eternally enjoyed together. Nikki felt a surge through her body as she contemplated how she would physically experience the love, wisdom, and power of God course through her entire being.

A Holy Bride

As God's glory fills the new heaven and earth, there is another important reality that appears amid God's majesty and love: "I saw the Holy City, the new Jerusalem, coming down out of heaven from God, prepared as a bride beautifully dressed for her husband. And I heard a loud voice from the throne saying, 'Look! God's dwelling place is now among the people, and he will dwell with them. They will be his people, and God himself will be with them and be their God'" (Revelation 21:2–3).

Here we see the Holy City, but the vision quickly shifts to a holy bride, beautifully dressed for her husband. At the beginning of God's story in the Old Testament, he described his promise of redemption in terms of a future marriage. Now here, in the last chapter of God's story, we see God fulfilling his covenant promise when Jesus Christ enters into marriage with his bride, the church.

The writer of the book of Revelation wants us to see and hear the ultimate reality of the age to come. He tells us that God "will dwell with them. They will be his people, and God himself will be with them and be their God" (21:3). On that day, we "will dwell in the house of the LORD forever" (Psalm 23:6).

In this new world of love, God will dwell in perfect unity with those he loves, and in response God's people will love him with all their heart, mind, soul, and strength. They will also love one another in ways that reflect how Jesus has loved them, helping each other to love God wholeheartedly.

A World of Perfection

The spiritual blessings that we have been given in Christ are not only for our present life but continue more fully into eternity. In the new heavens and new earth, our redemption will be complete, culminating with our complete sanctification and our consummated union with Christ.

Perfected Souls

In the Sermon on the Mount, Jesus says, "Blessed are the pure in heart, for they will see God" (Matthew 5:8). The Bible also says, "We know that when Christ appears, we shall be like him, for we shall see him as he is. All who have this hope in him purify themselves, just as he is pure" (1 John 3:2–3). It's a chicken-or-the-egg dilemma. We can only stand in God's holy presence in sinless perfection, but our hearts can only be made pure when we stand in Christ's presence. This mystery of transformation is impossible apart from God's power and grace.

When we stand in the *presence* of Jesus in the new creation, we will see his face and behold his glory. In that moment, he will fulfill his *promise* to complete the work he began in us (1 John 3:2; Philippians 1:6). By his glorious *power*, he will transform us into his own perfect image (2 Corinthians 3:18; Colossians 3:10).

When Mark reflected on these future realities, his heart and mind soared. He thought about what it will be like to no longer desire, or even have the capacity, to sin. He will no longer struggle with temptation, because God will have banished all evil from his kingdom. Mark's future hope makes him yearn to be free from sin's burdens and entanglements, but it also gives him the vision and motivation to live differently now. Though Mark knows he will still wrestle with sin, he also knows that he can experience more of God's love, joy, and peace as he abides with Christ on this side of heaven. God's bigger story gives hope for the future and strength for the present.

Perfected Bodies

The unfolding story of redemption not only gives hope for our souls but also offers redemption for our broken bodies. One day, God will transform our natural bodies into resurrected bodies. "The body that is sown is perishable, it is raised imperishable; it is sown in dishonor, it is raised in glory; it is sown in weakness, it is raised in power; it is sown a natural body, it is raised a spiritual body" (1 Corinthians 15:42–44). Our supernatural bodies will be free from disease, disorder, deformities, and limitations, enabling us to experience love, joy, and peace in infinitely greater and more profound ways.

Perfected Relationships

God will not only perfect our bodies and souls, but he will also perfect our relationships. The very communion we were created to have with God will finally be experienced perfectly and eternally. Let's imagine what that communion will be like.

We will know God perfectly, without any distortion or deficit. We will no longer need eyes of faith because "then we shall see face to face" (1 Corinthians 13:12). We will know his glory more fully, such that God's glory will be our glory and our glory will be God's glory. We will know the height, depth, width, and breadth of God's love personally because we will no longer battle any faith struggles.

Furthermore, *we will experience God's presence and power* in every fiber of our being. Seeing and experiencing God's glory will bring lasting change to our bodies and souls. In glory, there will no longer be any selfishness or sinfulness in our hearts and minds.

Experiencing God's perfect, life-sustaining love will obliterate any *fantasy* for something different from God. We will no longer experience any form of *anger* since we will experience perfect unity and peace with God and others in a place that is free of disaster, disease, and death. Because there will be no more loss of any kind, there will be no more *sorrow*. We will experience love, joy, and peace in ways that will satisfy our souls beyond measure, and as a result, we will never again struggle with *fear, shame, or guilt*. We will no longer deal with any common struggles.

Finally, *we will image God* perfectly since we will relate and respond to him without sin. God's love will fully rule our hearts so that we will relate to God totally out of a desire to please him, no longer tempted to live for ourselves. We will *relate* to others in ways motivated purely by love for God and love for them, where we consider them more important than ourselves. We will *respond* to God with perfect submission, which will result in perfect obedience through the power of God's Spirit. We will also *respond* to others exactly how God responds to each of us—with patience, kindness, goodness, faithfulness, gentleness, and self-control. We will no longer experience the pain of relational struggles.

Consummation brings complete restoration. Finally, our story will be completely redeemed by and aligned with God's story. More than ever, we can rejoice always, pray without ceasing, and give thanks in all circumstances. No fairy tale can compare to such an ending that marks the beginning of a never-ending life of love.

Love and Forgiveness in God's Story

After her intense afternoon of Bible study with Alice, Emma spent a lot of time reading, reflecting, and praying about her response to Steve. Emma knew she needed to forgive Steve, but she lacked the desire to restore her marriage relationship. If she took steps to reconcile with Steve and restore their relationship, she might set herself up for more hurt. Nevertheless, Emma focused on God's call to love and forgive like Christ. As she was wrestling with all that was going on in her heart, she knew she should not lean on her own understanding but rather trust God, who had been faithful during this season to give her wisdom and perspective from his Word.

In a recent sermon series at church, Emma's pastor had explained the gospel through God's grand narrative. He taught how the beginning and end of God's story—creation and consummation—serve as bookends that shape how we see, experience, and respond to life as we live in this broken world. Emma reviewed her notes from the series and thought about how love is the overarching theme in God's story. She considered the following points:

Creation shows us how God made us for love. Emma saw how this reality comes from the fact that God, who is love, created her in his image to reflect him through how she loves. We are commanded to love God and others (Matthew 22:37–40). As Jesus said, "Love one another. As I have loved you, so you must love one another" (John 13:34).

The Fall shows us that evil keeps us from love. As a result of the fall, we can love ourselves most instead of God. Emma saw how such self-love contributed to her marriage struggles with Steve. They had approached love as a transaction—loving on the basis of what they received from one another, what they thought the other deserved, and how they felt about the other. Emma now recognized how this self-centered love had disordered their souls and impacted their marriage. She also saw how she had placed her hopes and dreams of getting pregnant before her call to love God and Steve wholeheartedly.

Redemption shows us how Jesus restores us to love. Emma's pastor had explained how God sent the Son into our brokenness, because he knew that we could not rescue ourselves or fix our love problem. Emma now understood more than ever that Jesus loved her even when she was his enemy. She saw that God loved and forgave her despite her sinfulness and helplessness through Jesus's sacrificial death on the cross. She now understood that, given what he did for us, Jesus has every right to command us to love our enemies (Luke 6:27–36; Romans 5:10). Jesus was calling Emma to love Steve in the same way he has loved her. And if Jesus's sacrificial death for her wasn't enough motivation, God also poured out his love into her heart by his Spirit. Emma knew it would be impossible for her to love and forgive Steve in her own strength. Apart from Christ, her feelings and desires would not be enough, but she could love Steve with God's love even when she did not feel love for him. As a Christian, Emma is a new creation, and God has called her to be a minister of reconciliation and an ambassador for Christ (2 Corinthians 5:17–20).

Consummation shows us how we will enjoy love forever. As Emma reviewed the last sermon in her pastor's series and thought about the end of God's story, she remembered what he'd taught about enjoying perfect communion with God and perfect community with all of God's people. Emma knew that included Steve. Emma then thought about Steve's adultery within the lens of God's entire story. She knew that Jesus would change Steve's heart and fulfill his promise to complete the work he had begun. The question for Emma was whether she could wait on the Lord to do his faithful work, with no guarantee that she wouldn't be hurt again. She could reconcile with a perfected Steve in glory, but could she reconcile with an imperfect Steve now?

Emma decided that she would take one step of faith at a time. She responded to Steve's email, telling him that she would meet to hear what God had been doing in his heart. God's love compelled her to forgive Steve as Jesus had forgiven both her and Steve. Emma could envision reconciling with Steve as her brother in Christ, but she wasn't ready to consider restoring their marriage. Before taking those steps, she would wait and see how their meeting went.

In God's story, his forgiveness leads to our reconciliation and restoration. God desires intimacy with us. He is confident in his work of salvation, and he can be trusted. God not only gives us his Word to help us know how we should live, but he has given us himself—his presence, promises, and power fulfilled in his Son—so that we can live and love!

You Don't Have to Wait

You already have the privilege of living now as you will live forever. You can enjoy now what you will enjoy forever. The same God who will make consummation a reality is with you now. The same God who will wipe away every tear is the God "who comforts us in all our troubles" (2 Corinthians 1:3–4). You don't have to wait until heaven to know God and be changed by his unfailing love and glory. You don't have to wait until heaven to experience God's presence, promises, and power. You have full access now to your everlasting God through your union with Christ. God invites you to live fully in his story now, so that it can transform every aspect of your story.

You may think your struggles will never end. You can't imagine your future could be so beautiful. But God is restoring your soul and redeeming your story with every glimpse of Jesus and every step of faith. *Someday your journey through brokenness will end.* You will be fully formed in Christ—formed by his glory and for his glory. In the meantime, enjoy and respond to your Father's love. Draw near to the Son, who gives you rest. Be courageous and strong through the Spirit so that you don't grow weary and lose heart.

God's Invitation

Spend some time in God's Word. Open your heart to God by sharing your heart's response to the realities of the new heavens and earth.

Read Revelation 22:13–17 slowly once or twice. Consider Jesus's final invitation to abide in him until the end.

ACKNOWLEDGMENTS

I STAND humbled before and grateful to God for the wisdom he has entrusted to us through his gospel. Every time we journey with others through his story, I am amazed when we witness the breadth, width, height, and depth of his powerful love as he comforts his people and redeems their stories. Thank you, Lord, for your enduring faithfulness.

I am forever indebted to Karen, my loving wife, ministry companion, and prayerful encourager. *Restoration Story* and my other endeavors in life would not be complete without her perspective, insights, and experience. Thank you, Karen, for your steadfast love.

Our children: Ashley (Jesse), Ryan, and Whitney (Jerred), and adorable grandchildren: Asher, Rowan, Coraline, and Reagan have blessed me beyond measure. God has used them to grow me in ways I never dreamed. I can't imagine my story without them! Thank you, kids, for your precious hearts.

This work emerged and evolved through years of ministry at Sojourn Church Midtown. God has blessed me with exceptional friends in and around our Care ministry. Special shout-out to Nick Langford and Crystal Sridhar for hours of sacrificial interaction and Annie Kratzsch and

Jared Kennedy for their patient editorial work. Invaluable insight, testimonies, and feedback came from countless ministry leaders and participants within Midtown, across the country, and around the world. Thank you, friends, for your invaluable encouragement.

Finally, the vision for *Restoration Story* and the *Restore Study Guide* was set in motion after the initial breakfast conversation with Barbara Juliani and became a reality through the tireless work of New Growth Press. Thank you, team, for your faith-driven labor.

The whole is indeed more than the sum of its parts. But as I sit back and reflect, I praise God for the body of Christ and how its many members work together to craft the whole.

Indebted to love,
Robert K. Cheong

ENDNOTES

1. Duane A. Garrett, *Proverbs, Ecclesiastes, Song of Solomon*, New American Commentary, vol. 14 (Nashville: Broadman, 1993), 288.

2. Adapted from David Powlison, *Good & Angry: Redeeming Anger, Irritation, Complaining, and Bitterness* (Greensboro, NC: New Growth, 2016), 40.

3. A step-by-step guide for looking at your story can be found in the companion study guide, *Restore: Changing How We Live and Love* (Greensboro, NC: New Growth Press, 2020).

4. E. D. Hirsch, Jr., Joseph F. Kett, and James Trefil, eds. "Proverbs," *The New Dictionary of Cultural Literacy: What Every American Needs to Know* (New York: Houghton Mifflin Harcourt, 2002), 53.

5. "MACS0647-JD," updated July 21, 2020, *Wikipedia: The Free Encyclopedia*, https://en.wikipedia.org/wiki/MACS0647-JD/.

6. Davey Gott, "How Many Colors Are in the World?" *NCI News* (Winnipeg, Manitoba), May 3, 2019, https://www.ncifm.com/how-many-colors-are-there-in-the-world/.

7. Peter O'Brien, *Word Biblical Commentary: Colossians, Philemon*, ed. David A. Hubbard, Glenn W. Barker, vol. 44 (Waco, TX: Word, 1982), 47.

8. Gerald Bray, ed., *The Doctrine of the God: Contours of Christian Theology* (Downers Grove, IL: IVP, 1993), 92.

9. John Owens, *The Glory of Christ* (Carlisle, PA: Banner of Truth, 1994), 8.

10. Richard Lovelace, *Renewal as a Way of Life: A Guidebook for Spiritual Growth* (Eugene, OR: Wipf and Stock, 2002).

11. Adapted from David Powlison, *Good & Angry*, 40.

12. Philip Edgcumbe Hughes, *The New International Commentary on the New Testament: The Second Epistle to the Corinthians* (Grand Rapids, MI: Eerdmans, 1962), 57

13. Robert K. Cheong, *Restore Study Guide* (Greensboro, NC: New Growth, 2020), 93–99. Steps for reconciling broken relationships.

14. Charles Spurgeon, *Spurgeon's Expository Encyclopedia* (Grand Rapids, MI: Baker, 2006), 321.

15. John Piper, "Why Did Jesus Cry, 'My God, My God, Why Have You Forsaken Me?'" *Desiring God* (website), March 1, 2016, www.desringgod.org/interviews/my-god-my-god-why-have-you-forsaken-me-didnt-jesus-already-know.

16. Peter J. Gentry and Stephen J. Wellum, *God's Kingdom through God's Covenant: A Concise Biblical Theology* (Wheaton IL: Crossway, 2015), 17, 56.

THE RESTORE STUDY GUIDE

THE COMPANION study guide (*Restore: Changing How We Live and Love* (New Growth Press, 2020) will help you to more fully examine and process your story. While the concepts are the same, the study guide will help you to work through your story in light of God's story.

You can also use the workbook in group settings to take the journey together. You will learn and grow with one another, and you'll discover that your relationships with your friends will deepen as you listen to one another's stories and struggles.

Check out our website www.gospel.care to see how churches across the country and the world are using *Restore* to help God's people grow confident in Jesus Christ through his Word and his story.